ER

Cover: the author in 1990, aged 76

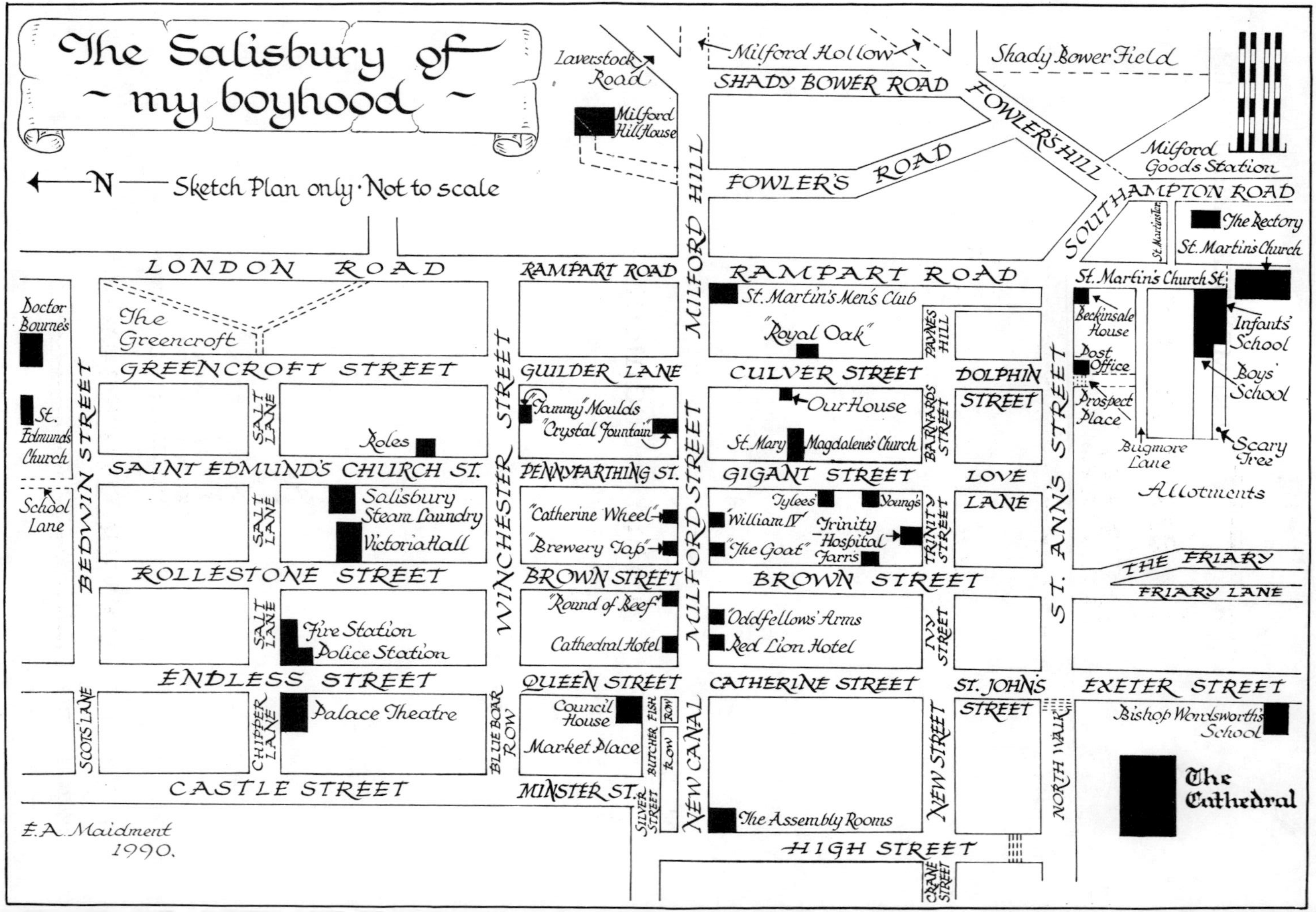
The Salisbury of
~ my boyhood ~
N
Sketch Plan only · Not to scale
Laverstock Road
Milford Hill House
Milford Hollow
Shady Bower Field
SHADY BOWER ROAD
FOWLER'S HILL
FOWLER'S ROAD
Milford Goods Station
SOUTHAMPTON ROAD
The Rectory
St. Martin's Church
MILFORD HILL
LONDON ROAD
RAMPART ROAD
RAMPART ROAD
St. Martin's Church St.
St. Martin's Men's Club
"Royal Oak"
PAYNES HILL
Beckinsale House
Infants' School
Post Office
Boys' School
Prospect Place
Bugmore Lane
Scary Tree
Allotments
Doctor Bourne's
The Greencroft
GREENCROFT STREET
GUILDER LANE
CULVER STREET
DOLPHIN STREET
St. Edmund's Church
SALT LANE
Roles
"Tammy" Moulds
"Crystal Fountain"
Our House
St. Mary Magdalene's Church
BARNARDS STREET
SAINT EDMUND'S CHURCH ST.
PENNYFARTHING ST.
GIGANT STREET
LOVE LANE
School Lane
Salisbury Steam Laundry
Victoria Hall
"Catherine Wheel"
"Brewery Tap"
Tylees'
Young's
"William IV"
Trinity Hospital
"The Goat"
Farrs
TRINITY STREET
ST. ANN'S STREET
THE FRIARY
FRIARY LANE
BEDWIN STREET
ROLLESTONE STREET
WINCHESTER STREET
BROWN STREET
MILFORD STREET
BROWN STREET
"Round of Beef"
Cathedral Hotel
"Oddfellows' Arms
Red Lion Hotel
IVY STREET
Fire Station
Police Station
ENDLESS STREET
QUEEN STREET
CATHERINE STREET
ST. JOHN'S STREET
EXETER STREET
SCOTS LANE
CHIPPER LANE
Palace Theatre
BLUE BOAR ROW
Council House
Market Place
BUTCHER ROW
FISH ROW
NEW CANAL
NEW STREET
NORTH WALK
Bishop Wordsworth's School
The Cathedral
CASTLE STREET
MINSTER ST.
SILVER STREET
The Assembly Rooms
HIGH STREET
CRANE STREET
E.A. Maidment
1990.

I remember
I REMEMBER

The Story of my Boyhood in Salisbury

Arthur Maidment

Arthur Maidment

BAVERSTOCK BOOKS

Published 1990 by
Baverstock Books
50 Westbury Leigh
Westbury
Wiltshire

Origination and design by Ex Libris Press
1 The Shambles
Bradford on Avon
Wiltshire

Typeset by Manuscript, Trowbridge

Printed by BPCC Wheatons, Ltd., Exeter

ISBN 0 9516759 0 7

ACKOWLEDGEMENTS

I am indebted to the many people who have helped in the publication of this book and would especially thank my son and daughter-in-law Mr & Mrs G.A.M.Maidment, my daughter and son-in-law Mr & Mrs J.Cox-Maidment, Mrs D.Adcock, Mrs Bean, Mrs Conduit, Mr P.Daniels, Mr D.Eidelstein, Mr & Mrs A.Feltham, Miss A.Hodder, Mr R.Jones, Mrs Molly Maidment, Mr R.Newman, Mr & Mrs Reason, Mr J.Russ, Mr W.Sanders, Mrs P.Sharp, Mrs B.Sobucinska and Mr L.G.Tolley.

CONTENTS

This book is dedicated to my wife

Madge

who told me so many times in the years before her death —
"Write your memories down before it's too late".
So here they are and I hope that you may find something that will trigger a memory from your own times past.

Thomas Moore, the poet wrote:-

Oft in the stilly night,
Ere slumbers chains have bound me;
Fond memory brings the light,
Of other days around me;
The smiles the tears,
Of boyhood's years ......

PREFACE

I think that before starting on the memories of my own life, it would be as well to say something about my ancestors.

My father's family came from the south-west Wiltshire/north Dorset area. In the last century Maidment was a very common name in that part of the country, especially in the villages of Semley, Donhead Saint Mary, Donhead Saint Andrew, Sedgehill, East and West Knoyle and Tisbury. Early in that century, several Maidments were trading in the small town of Mere. Dad was born in Donhead Saint Mary in June of 1882, but spent several years of his boyhood in Semley where, although no Maidments can be found in the village today, in 1851 it possessed more than twenty families with the name.

During the past few years, my daughter Pamela has been researching the family and has been successful in tracing back to the marriage of William Maidment to Mary Gray on 16th November 1805. The record in Semley Register is most interesting, for it shows that William signed in rather hesitant fashion, as though it was a real effort; his surname started with a small m, his bride made her mark, but one of the witnesses, Joseph Maidment, signed in a beautiful copperplate.

My grandmother Maidment was born a Maidment and truly defied the old saying — "Change the name and not the letter; change for worse and not for better" as she did not even change her name. Her mother, who had been born Charlotte Davis in France in 1815, married Samuel Maidment at Donhead Saint Mary on 20th December 1837. Both husband and wife signed the register in well-formed copperplate; this was not surprising for Great-Grandmother was the Semley schoolmistress and doubtless saw to it that Samuel's signature was up to scratch.

Dad's family moved around the area during his boyhood — he could remember living at Cann, near Shaftesbury; Pentridge; East Stour;

Charlton-All-Saints and Downton after leaving Semley, where they had moved from his birthplace of Donhead Saint Mary. They arrived in Salisbury in the middle of the eighteen-nineties, for Dad finished his schooling at St. Martin's, before becoming an apprentice coachsmith to Mr. Frank Cooper in Brown Street at a starting wage of one shilling and sixpence per week.

At Easter, 1950, I took my father back to the area, the first time that he had returned. Finding our way along the country lanes was quite a problem as the signposts removed during the invasion scare of 1940 were still missing. However, we came to the top of a hill and Dad said, "I think that's Semley down in the valley."

Just then we saw a very old countryman making his way home. My father wound the window down and asked if we were on the road to Semley. The old chap said yes and enquired who we wanted to see. Dad said that he had lived there as a boy.

"What be your name then?"

"Maidment."

The old gentleman looked hard at Dad, then said,

"I 'low you be one of Cordelia Maidment's boys."

My father, who died just over a year later, was astounded that the family should be remembered almost sixty years after leaving the village.

My own ego was somewhat dented in 1980 during a visit to Tisbury during a Saturday afternoon in the summer. My wife Madge went into a shop with a young friend who was staying with us while I continued strolling down the street and saw the Vicar sitting at a table in a shop doorway, collecting for the Church Roof fund. When I stopped and gave him some money, he said,

"You're not from these parts."

I replied that my family had lived in the area at the end of the last century.

"What name"

"Maidment"

"That's not a family, that's a tribe."

Mum's family, the Tappers, had lived in Salisbury for generations. The history of St. Martin's Church records William Tapper as Church Warden in 1723 and 1724.

My Great-Grandfather Tapper who was born in Greencroft Street,

Salisbury in 1787, served in the Peninsular War from 1808 to 1814 and I still possess his Campaign Medal complete with four bars. When he was just twenty-one years of age, he was a member of the Local Yeomanry who were called upon to provide a troop for Spain. The members cast lots as to who should go, and though great-grandfather drew a blank, he was dazzled by the gold offered by a colleague, William Bird Brodie, and somewhat foolishly took his place. Off he went, probably envisaging a few months away at most, then found himself in Spain for six long years. He took part in four decisive battles, Talavera, Badajoz, Vittoria and Toulouse — as a member of The 14th Light Dragoons. The battle at Badajoz in 1812 is looked upon as one of the bloodiest in the history of the British Army. It lasted for twenty days, five thousand British were killed, thousands more were wounded. Even "The Iron Duke" Wellington wept at the horrendous casualties and when, after the final taking of the citadel, his troops went on the rampage in a drunken state, he said, "Let them have their fun." Shocked by the slaughter, the troops shot the men, raped the women, even nuns, and bayonetted children. It was forty-eight hours before order was restored and off went the army to finish the job which took two more years.

Great-Grandfather returned home to marry his sweetheart and somewhat late in his life my grandfather, John, was born in 1835.

Meanwhile William Bird Brodie who paid him to take his place, made the most of the time which he had purchased. Brodie, the son of the Rector of Winterslow, bought later in 1808, in conjunction with two friends, John Dowding and John Luxford, The Salisbury and Winchester Journal, which had previously belonged to his uncle, Benjamin Collins. He then also started a bookshop, this was followed by the formation of Brodie's Bank. By 1812, he was chosen as Mayor of the City, then in 1833, immediately after the Reform Act, became Member of Parliament for Salisbury immediately after The Reform Act, an office which he held for thirteen years. Then came a change in his fortunes, for Brodie's Bank collapsed and he retired to spend the rest of his life in Swanage, a ruined man.

Saddened by the depravations of his men during the Napoleonic War, in 1816 the Officer Commanding, 14th Light Dragoons, approached the Pope, asking for absolution. This was granted, the Pontiff ordering that for the next 101 years, the regiment's band should play his favourite hymn, "Vespers", each Tuesday and Thursday morning.

It is incredible that today, some 176 years later, this custom is still being observed by The Dragoons successors, The 14th/20th Kings Hussars.

1 *My Early Years*

I was born on 22nd September 1914, just seven weeks after the outbreak of the First World War, at number fifty Culver Street in Salisbury, but before I reached my first birthday, the family had moved into the house next door, number forty-eight, and it was there that I spent the next twenty-one years of my life.

Culver Street was one of the original streets of The City of New Sarum (the official name for Salisbury) which had been laid out in the Roman grid pattern. It was first mentioned in the City archives in 1402 as Melmonger or Culver Street. "Mell" was the Anglo-Saxon name for honey, so presumably a Melmonger was a honey seller. Culver, the Anglo-Saxon name for a wood-pigeon, was still in common usage in the latter part of the eighteenth century.

The hundred or so houses in the street were a heterogeneous collection which I imagine were built between 1700 and 1890 to replace much earlier dwellings. The population in 1914 was probably about the five hundred mark, the breadwinners having a multitude of occupations, clerks, craftsmen of many types, labourers, gardeners, drovers, engine drivers and other railway workers, cab drivers and even one lamplighter. Not many wives had full time jobs although some were laundry workers and a number were employed part-time as cleaners.

Most houses were lit by gas but many still relied on oil lamps and candles. Street lighting was from flickering gas lamps on cast-iron standards some ten feet high and dating from early Victorian times. The road was still impacted gravel and during the summer months the Corporation water cart, drawn by massive horses, made frequent visits in a not altogether successful attempt to lay the constant dust. Rubbish was collected weekly by another horse-drawn vehicle, a high-sided open cart — not a very hygienic method!

Each day, one of the City's policemen would put in an appearance, slowly and ponderously plodding his beat, having a word with most people who seemed to miss very little. The threat, "I'll tell the policeman", was usually enough to put the fear of God into most children who knew that the men in blue were quite capable of summary justice on the spot — the boxing of ears.

The Salisbury into which I was born was a world apart from the present city. Generally speaking, there was a shortage of money, holidays were almost unknown, but the street had a community spirit seldom found today. There were instances of neighbours whose families had lived next to each other for several generations and willing help was always forthcoming in times of trouble. I think the main difference was that people had roots — unlike today when many have to move on after a couple of years and have the problem of making a new home, time and time again, during the course of a working life.

Memory is a wonderful thing and it is amazing just how far back one can remember. Little incidents stand out and I often wonder why. No doubt, everything that one has ever experienced is tucked away in the brain but the problem is recall which seems to be triggered by a sight, a sound or a smell.

When I was very small, my father used to perch me on his knee, but always I wanted to get down as soon as possible, the reason was the horrible smell from his nicotine stained fingers. Dad could never afford to be a heavy smoker but inadvertently he instilled in me a lifelong aversion to tobacco. Poor Dad, I expect he often wondered why his only son didn't want to stay on his knee.

The time came when, being two and a half years of age and to my mind quite grown up, I felt that I had outgrown my mailcart. What was a mailcart? Simply a wicker pram, so called because, between 1870 to 1920, postmen did their rounds pushing wicker baskets on wheels. Hence a wicker pram was dubbed a mailcart. One morning Mum got mine out and off down Culver Street we went, with me marching proudly at the side. Proud because Mum had told me that we were giving the thing away and so never again would I have to ride in it. We reached the end of the street, crossed Milford Street into Guilder Lane and on to the empty premises of The Rainbow Laundry, where all sorts of items were being collected for the relief of those fleeing from the German air raids on London.

Another quite vivid memory from round about this time is watching the removal of a boiler from the same Rainbow Laundry. It seemed to be absolutely huge and was edged slowly onto a large waggon drawn by four big cart horses. The incident probably stands out because of the shouting that went on during what must have been a major operation as only muscle power was available.

During the summer of 1917, my mother took me on a Mothers' Union Outing to Milford-on-Sea by a horse-drawn waggonette, which had seats on either side, with curtains that could be drawn, both at sides and back. The changing of horses at Downton and looking out through the back curtains as we left that village whilst the poor horses made the long and steep ascent of Lode Hill are still fresh in my mind. I remember hoping that the waggonette would not run backwards down the hill. Whether I went to sleep shortly after this, I don't know, but I cannot recall the rest of the day.

From the time that I started at St. Martin's Infants' School at the age of three, on Thursday afternoons I had to make my way to St. Martin's Mens Club where the Parish Branch of the Mothers' Union held its meetings. I used to shyly push open the door, look around and as soon as I spotted Mum make a mad dash to her; I was probably cosseted and these meetings were always enjoyable because I was given cakes — what small boy can resist freshly baked home-make cakes. My father never could, even in his sixties. Once, on my way to the meeting, a girl in my class named Marjorie Offer, tagged along with me. When we arrived at the clubroom, she announced to her mother, so that all could hear, that I was her sweetheart. Bloomin' cheek — I didn't even like her very much. I was most embarrassed — probably went red as beetroot and all shy for the rest of the afternoon.

My Aunt Gertrude, who lived with us, was a very sweet lady — for many years she worked at Nelson House, one of the Godolphin School Boarding Houses. She often took me out on Wednesdays which was her half-day off and on one occasion, when I was very young, we went to a First Aid Display in The Bishop's Palace given by Boy Scouts and Girl Guides. Whilst I only have vague memories of the display, I do recall my excitement at the sight of the lake with an island in the middle and wishing I could paddle and play there. It seemed a vast expanse of water but the next time that I saw it a few years later I found that it was really only a large pond — when you are small everything seems bigger.

Few people today remember the old Assembly Rooms at the corner of New Canal and High Street in Salisbury. I was only a tiny lad when all the family — my father, mother, two sisters and I — went there to see a variety show, sitting in the back row. As I couldn't see the stage, boredom set in and I suppose I made a nuisance of myself. Dad had a great idea and sat me up on the very wide window sill behind the seating. Although this gave me the best seat in the house, it wasn't long before I went to sleep right there and allowed the rest to have some peace.

At about the same time that I started at St. Martin's Infants' School in September 1917 I also commenced Sunday School which was held in the same building and run by Miss Mangin, the elderly spinster daughter of a former Rector. She lived in a largish house for those days in St. Martin's Church Street, only about a hundred yards away from the Church. There was a sort of dogleg in the building line at this point which led to the pavement being very wide — it was constructed of extremely old and well worn slabs, some of which were the most unusual colour of pale blue. After Sunday School we used to be taken into church for part of the Evensong Service and on one occasion everything had to take place early as no lights could be switched on, owing to the introduction of the blackout and the fear of air raids. I have since learnt that this event was early autumn 1917.

Another early memory is the dedication of the beautifully carved rood screen at St. Martin's Church early in 1918. It had been erected to the memory of Lieutenant Rawlings who had been killed in 1915 on the Western Front. The father, Mr. Rawlings, a former captain of the City Volunteer Fire Brigade, was the founder of Rawlings The Furnishers of Blue Boar Row and Endless Street where the firm traded for almost a century.

The mind of a child can conjure up all sorts of things and as the screen was unveiled I thought that the intricately carved squares at the three top ends of the crucifix were like custard cream biscuits. Every time that I looked at the screen in the years that followed I thought my first impression was apt. I expect the wonderful craftsman who produced this beautiful work would have had his ego badly dented by the thoughts of a small boy.

The first aeroplane that I saw is firmly etched in my mind. My mother and I were in the garden of our Culver Street home when this huge monster flew over very low — probably 2-300 feet. Mum and Mrs. Bruton, her neighbour, were talking about it and I learned that it was a Handley-Page Bomber. They knew — because of its swept back wings — and I have often wondered how two housewives had gleaned such highly technical knowledge.

The winter of 1917/18 saw a severe shortage of food. One morning on hearing that a supply of butter had arrived, Mum dispatched my elder sister, with me in tow, to The Maypole in Silver Street. We joined a long, long queue and it seemed hours before we even reached the shop. On arrival there, I was intrigued by the mosaic floor which had the name Maypole as part of the design. As far as the butter was concerned we were out of luck — the last of the supply was sold just before it was our turn.

When food was dreadfully short, a communal Soup Kitchen was set up in the Lear Memorial Rooms in Gigant Street. We went along with basins and were served from a tap which was at the end of a pipe coming through the wall into the street where trestle tables had been erected.

Our house was only about 150 yards away from Gibbs Mew's Brewery and every morning at midday a wonderful malty smell would emanate from there. At the same time the brewery chimney used to belch white smoke and Mum always said, "They've just mixed the brew."

Whatever the reason I still recall with pleasure that lovely aroma though, strangely, never became a beer drinker.

During the spring of 1918, my sisters with some of their friends and I went for a walk along the Lime Kilns — that's Bishopdown, and someone said that if you put your ear to the ground it was possible to hear the guns firing on the front in France. So we all tried it and I am still wondering if the rumble I heard really was the sound of guns some 150 miles away. It is possible, because it is recorded that the sound of the Venesta Factory Explosion in London was heard in Salisbury. Although the factory was destroyed, the vibration could hardly have been as great as that caused by 10,000 heavy guns being fired during the German push of 1918.

I think it was indeed fortunate that one of my unmarried aunts lived with us, as it led to many more interesting outings than might otherwise have come my way. On a glorious summer afternoon, Aunt Gertrude took me to visit Mrs. Hobbs, grandmother's cousin who lived at Downton. Such a trip in 1918 was infinitely more thrilling than the modern child would have today — for them a seven mile car ride — for me a trip by steam train. First the long walk to the South Western Railway Station — anticipation probably easing tired legs — then through the ticket barrier onto Platform 1, which was always reserved for the Bournemouth train. The excitement, the smell of smoke and steam as we passed through the London Road Tunnel just outside the station, the wonderful open farmland after leaving Alderbury Junction and, finally, the narrow dark tunnel just before arriving at Downton. Yes, the 1918 trip had much to commend it.

Mrs. Hobbs lived in a tiny cottage in the Manor House grounds just off Barford Lane — a walk of some 3-400 yards from the station. I remember going into the house and thinking it strange to see a fire burning on such a hot day. At home, the summer cooking was done by gas, but what can beat the homely smell of a wood fire? After tea I wandered off through the gate to The Manor House, then through another gate into the churchyard where the grass seemed like a jungle and was almost tall enough to hide a small boy. Suddenly I was missed but after a long search Mrs. Hobbs found me and then had to spend a considerable time deciphering the inscriptions on the tombstones for me. In 1985 I revisited the cottage and was delighted to find it unaltered and just as I remembered.

It was probably around this time that the family used to go up to the Railway Station on Sunday afternoons to watch the War Wounded arrive by Ambulance Train. Dad had lost the sight of his right eye in an industrial accident in 1915 whilst making Field Kitchens for the Canadian Army and this fact, plus having a job of National Importance, had kept him from joining the Armed Forces. Since very early in the war he had been a member of the Salisbury Division Red Cross Voluntary Aid Detachment, part of whose job was to ferry the wounded from the train to the various military hospitals in the district.

One of the station trips stands out in my mind. When we arrived the Red Cross personnel — my father amongst them — were sitting on milk churns in the Station Yard, taking the weight off their feet as many of them had probably been on duty at the Infirmary during the previous night. The Motor Ambulances, with canvas hoods and bright Red Cross insignia, were lined up in readiness but we learned from Dad that

The Salisbury Division Red Cross Voluntary Aid Detachment pictured outside the Salisbury General Infirmary.

the train would be very late in arriving. When eventually it did draw in, the scene changed as everything was done at the double. The Red Cross VADs went into the station in pairs with stretchers, then came out at a slow trot with the wounded on board, pop them into the waiting ambulances, then return for another poor chap. It was all done very smartly and efficiently, even seen through the eyes of a small boy. Looked at in retrospect, it may seem rather macabre to spend a Sunday afternoon watching the wounded arrive, but I suppose people wanted to show sympathy and welcome them home.

Sometime during the summer of 1918, my two sisters and I — in the care of Aunt Gertrude — set out for a picnic on Laverstock Down. On the way we stopped at The Godolphin School Gardener's Cottage in Laverstock Road where we were joined by the gardener's wife, Mrs. Brooks, and their daughter Jessie, who was at The Bishop Wordsworth's School with my elder sister. In 1918, apart from the Brooks House and The Lodge Cottage at Laverstock Hall, there were no houses between Millbrook and Laverstock Mill — a distance of about half-a-mile. The village itself was sparsely populated and so the walk to the Down seemed a long, long way to a three — well, nearly four-year-old. It seemed quite an adventure. We stopped for the picnic at the brick platform that was used for many years by the Territorial Army when firing at the Rifle Range Targets further up the hill. Mrs. Brooks had taken a kettle so we collected sticks for a fire. This was soon done and in no time the first camp fire that I had seen was blazing away merrily. It was a lovely afternoon. Unfortunately Jessie Brooks died a year or so later. I remember her as a kind girl.

Her father Mr. Brooks was a real character — he was a big heavy man, had a very gruff voice, side whiskers and a large moustache. He always wore an outsize floppy trilby hat. His feet can only be described as plates of meat — that he was a martyr to corns was no secret — Dad had a regular assignment to cut them for him. The corns were probably a legacy from his lifetime of gardening. He must have been a very good gardener because his cottage walls were filled with framed prize certificates from numerous Horticultural Shows. Dad was always getting tips from him on gardening — tips which were worth while because Mr. Brooks was quite a sage. There were some four or five undergardeners also employed; they not only supplied School House with fruit and vegetables but also kept the playing fields, tennis courts and the many hedges in first class order.

Accompanying Dad and Mr. Brooks on an inspection tour of the gardens was a pleasurable experience as we always finished up at the apple store and needless to say I never left empty handed. On one such tour, when I was quite small I really let the side down by asking,

"Dad, why does Mr. Brooks keep making rude noises?"

Neither Mr. Brooks nor Dad said a word, but on the way home it was drummed into me that you never made comments like that.

Armistice Day, 1918, is a very clear memory. By coincidence it was St. Martin's Day — a big day in the life of those attending, as I did, St. Martin's School. I had been told that after going to school we would all go over to the Church and at the end of a special service the rest of the day would be a holiday. I must have gone off to school on that fateful Monday morning in pleasurable anticipation. We duly went into church at 10 o'clock and the Rector, Reverend Ian Grant Cameron went up into the pulpit to tell us that, at 11 o'clock, the war would be over. We then sang one hymn, followed by "God Save The King"; then we were free to go home. Excited people were rushing about, there was lots of shouting going on and, to my embarrassment I was picked up to be hugged and kissed by a lady who was a complete stranger.

Shortly after I got home Dad arrived with a large Union Jack which he had borrowed and proceeded to look for a flag pole. Unfortunately his eye (he only had one) alighted on a bamboo curtain pole about two inches in diameter, and he put the flag on this. He went upstairs to the front bedroom on the second floor with me just behind and fixed the flag to the window sill where it hung beautifully over the street. The two four inch nails which he had grabbed in his haste split the wood and, end of the war or not Mum was quite cross with him, but she never stayed cross for long. After dinner, my two sisters took me up to Victoria Park where there were swings and a seesaw and a giant's stride. Unfortunately it was not a happy afternoon for me. Someone had given me tuppence, so on the way I went into Mrs. Goodfellow's Newsagents Shop at the corner of Milford Street and Gigant Street to buy a cap pistol for three ha'pence and a round box of caps for a ha'penny. Shortly afterwards my joy turned to tears when I pinched in the pistol the loose skin between my thumb and forefinger on the right hand resulting in a big red blister.

Just after Armistice Day an event without precedent took place in Salisbury during our School Christmas Holidays.

South Wiltshire was at that time one vast army camp — there were even bell tents on Bishopdown — the troops were fed up — the war was over and all they wanted was to get back home, none more so than the well-paid Australians. One Sunday evening the City Police, who must have had a terrible job, arrested three of them for drunkenness and put them in the cells for the night. The Police Station was at that time quite a small building situated at the corner of Endless Street and Salt Lane. Needless to say the colleagues of the arrested Aussies, who were probably in a right old mood before arrival in the City, refused to take events lying down, so they rioted, broke every window in the building, smashed down the doors, forced their way into the cells and released them.

Next morning the City was agog with the news and my sisters took me along to Endless Street which was thronged with people. I can still see in my mind the damage that had been caused and the Chief Constable, Mr. Frank Richardson walking in the street, still wearing a bloodstained bandage around his head rather like a turban.

It was not long after this that the Aussies took their departure and

I have a vivid recollection of a Monday morning a few weeks later, being awakened to say goodbye to two of my cousins — sisters who had both married soldiers from the Dominion and were following their husbands to make a new life on the other side of the world. Mum said, "I don't suppose you'll ever see them again", but I did when they both came back as old ladies some fifty years later.

During the period after the Armistice and on into early 1919 the terrible 'flu epidemic was raging. More died from this scourge than were killed in the war. My eldest sister caught it and was quite ill, but my mother stated categorically that she was alright and wouldn't die because she had had a nose bleed. As with so many things, Mum was again correct, but the churchyards around Salisbury, especially to the West, bear witness to the severity of the outbreak. Rows of white headstones remembering the troops — mostly colonial — who did not live to make the journey back home.

In the summer of 1919, the body of Lieutenant Rawlings, in whose memory the rood screen had been erected at St. Martin's was brought back to be re-interred in the churchyard of St. Andrew's, Laverstock. This must have been during a school holiday because my sisters took me along to see the military funeral. The coffin was carried on a horse drawn gun-carriage and the burial took place on the north side of the little church, after which the escort fired three volleys over the grave.

One afternoon there was great excitement — we all rushed to St. Ann's Street to see a tank which had just arrived at Milford Station, ponderously make its way to Victoria Park. It had been given to the City to mark the great efforts made during the various War Weapons Weeks. On arrival at the park it was driven onto a concrete base which had been prepared behind the Sports Pavilion — not a very prominent place for display. There it stayed, getting more and more rusty by the year until in the early 1940s it was taken for scrap to help fight the second World War. In the interim the tank provided a wonderful plaything for small boys who never tired of clambering over the monster.

On Saturday, 26th July, 1919, a Peace Tea was held for the Infants School Children of the City. The venue was Doctor Bourne's field at the rear of Saint Edmund's College — now the District Council Office. Every child in our school had a drum and we practised beating in rhythm for days beforehand. Dad told me to march like a soldier —

eyes front all the time — he should have said sailor for I remember wearing my sailor suit — they were much in fashion at that period. We marched from School — along St. Martin's Church Street, down St. Ann's Street, then right turn into Dolphin Street and so to Culver Street where I lived. All the people were standing at the front doors, attracted by the steady beat of the drums. As I got closer to my home, I could see Dad, Mum, my two sisters and Mr. Bussell, a workmate of Dad's who had just been demobbed and was staying with us for a short while, standing at the door. Remembering Dad's instructions I ignored them — eyes front and on I marched beating away. I was quite disgusted when my friend Frank Gurd who was marching next to me shouted out "Hello, Mrs. Maidment." As I remember the tea it was a very tame affair; we seemed to wait for ages for something to happen — eventually food was served: we only got one cake each and that was the end of the day.

The Peace Pageant for the remainder of the schools was held on the following Monday, July 28th, the theme being the City's history. There

The Peace Pageant of 28th July, 1919.

was a magnificent procession and all the schools took part headed by the Salisbury Giant and Hobnob. I remember being quite scared when the latter ran towards where we were standing in Queen Street. The Bishop Wordsworth's School looked really smart — boys in white flannels and white shirts, the girls (yes the school did have girls until 1927) in white blouses and navy blue skirts. The school must have had a lot of practice in marching — I remember Dad saying how good they were — he was probably biased as my sister was among the girls on parade.

On arrival at Victoria Park, the schools performed tableaux representing the major events of the city's past. Mr. Windust, St. Martin's Deputy Headmaster, played the part of Father Time — between the tableaux a trumpet was sounded and he made a pass with his scythe representing another century or so passing. I asked what he was doing and, on being told, was rather frightened as to what might happen if he miscounted and went beyond the present century.

The St. Martin's School tableau represented the building of the present cathedral by Bishop Poore. It is interesting to note that the part of the famous bishop was actually played by Robert Poore who lived at the first house in Exeter Street. The members of the family were for evermore known as Bishie Poore.

During the 1919 Summer holidays — my sisters and I in the care of my aunt went for a week's holiday at Lower Parkstone, staying with a relative of a relative! The house, compared with home, seemed rather up-market even boasting a side entrance with its own gate. We seemed to spend ages going to and from Bournemouth by tram. I remember the super toy shop right by the pier. One event during the week was quite exciting when the boy of the house, who was about my age, got himself lost. The police were informed and they advised my aunt to go back to Parkstone; this we did but in the meantime all sorts of things went through my mind — would he starve? — could the gypsies have taken him? However, we had hardly got back to the house when the boy arrived under police escort. Another panic over.

During the summer of 1919, as a result of a rabies outbreak in London, dogs had to wear muzzles, something which made each and every one of them look very fierce.

An exciting family event took place during the late autumn of that year. My father went to London for a week-end — his first holiday since his marriage in 1904. He stayed with his old workmate, Bill Barron who, like Dad, had been apprenticed with Frank Cooper, the Coachbuilder of Brown Street. In 1908 Bill had foreseen the future for aviation and had gone to Hendon, where his coachbuilding skills were put to work building planes. About a year afterwards he endeavoured to persuade Dad to follow but the chance was too great for a married man with two children — a decision that I am sure my father regretted as the years passed and he saw his former workmate become more and more prosperous.

A few weeks previously Mum and Dad decided that he must have a new overcoat for the big occasion, and so on a Sunday afternoon the whole family walked up past the Great Western Railway Station to Windsor Road where the tailor lived. At this time Salisbury had many bespoke tailors, multiple shops only arrived in the thirties. Dad walked on in front but I wasn't going to be left out, ran after him and he relented and let me accompany him. The tailor — Mr. Vincent — was a tall, rather austere man, sporting a waxed moustache, much in vogue at that time. My father said that he wanted a navy blue coat — Mr. Vincent pulled down a roll of cloth from shelves near the window of the front room which was his workshop. I remember him saying that it was a first class cloth and did Dad want a velvet collar? Then Dad was measured for the new coat — the purchase of which must have been quite an expense.

When the big day arrived Dad came home to tea at the usual time and was due to catch the 7.30 train. It meant that he only lost the Saturday morning–time lost meant wages lost. It was the first time that I had known him go away; as the idea didn't go down very well with me he tried bribery and gave me tuppence to go and buy a comic. I ran off down the street but, after about thirty yards, I tripped, the tuppence rolled out of my hand and down a shallow rainwater drain. I went back home in tears and although Dad must have been short of time, he still got the acetylene lamp off his bike and we went to look for the lost coins but in vain. He then took me with him as he made his way to the station, went into Mrs. Goodfellow's newsagents shop, bought the comic and left me to make my way home.

It really was a long week-end and it seemed ages before he came back with presents for everyone. There was a stamp album for my eldest sister, a book called "Queensland Cousins" for my other sister and a three tier pencil box for me. The stamp album was passed down through the family as was the book which I still have. However, I'm afraid that the pencil box did not have such a long life-span; I've no idea what eventually happened to it.

During my early years I accumulated a deal of local knowledge from my mother whose family had lived in the city for many generations. One of her favourite expressions was "They say", though she never explained who "They" were. No doubt she was referring to her own father and mother who had in their turn received the information via their own parents and so on. I remember Mum telling me the origin of the carvings which are part of The Close Wall in Exeter Street — "They say they came from the Cathedral at Old Sarum." Absolutely right! She pointed out "The Wyndham Memorial" just inside and to the right of the present Cathedral's West Door where Lady Wyndham is depicted minus one finger. "They say she caught the plague, everyone thought she was dead and, as she lay in her coffin, a manservant cut off her finger to steal her rings. Mrs. Wyndham was only in a coma and the shock revived her." A compelling story, probably passed down through generations but was it true?

Mum also pointed out "The Salisbury Pig' in one of the Purbeck Marble pillars standing outside and to the left of the Cathedral's West Door. I have showed this, in my turn, to my own children and to dozens of other kiddies. The pig still looks as though he's running away.

2 *Saint Martin's Infants*

A week or so before my third birthday I started school at Saint Martin's Mixed Infants. This was situated about fifteen yards from the Church at the end of Saint Martin's Church Street, which then was still connected to Saint Ann's Street. At the corner was Beckingsale House, a corrective training establishment for "bad girls", as my mother explained to me. Unfortunately she did not explain what a "bad girl" was. I had reached my early teens before I found out.

The Infants' School was next to the one catering for the seven to fourteen year olds, which at the time that I started school in 1917 was still for boys and girls. However, in 1920, the girls were transferred to The George Herbert School in Milford Street whilst the boys from that school went to Saint Martins.

My earliest recollection of the Infants' School is of the massive rocking horse, just inside the street door. It was the old fashioned sort with real rockers and I wondered, would I be expected to ride such a giant. My fears were groundless as it was seldom used. Another early memory is of the really scary tree at the bottom of the playground, that was usually marshy in winter, being almost down to the level of the River Avon flowing some two hundred yards away. The tree was a skeleton which having been dead for many years, was bleached almost white and presented a frightening sight to toddlers. Why those in authority allowed it to stay is beyond me.

The school had a very long room, which was divided by sliding screens built of wood with obscured glass windows at the top. To the end of this room was the toddlers' classroom which was unusual for it had a well running down the centre and to left and right were three tiers rising on each side. At the far end of this room were double doors leading to a lobby which in turn had doors to the playground. This had a buttressed brick wall on three sides, dividing it from the old churchyard on the left, the "big school" to the right and allotments at the bottom.

A week or so after starting school, I suppose the novelty had worn off for on the way back one afternoon, I announced to Mum that I didn't want to go. As she insisted, I had a few tears, whereupon she said, "Lets go back home". Just before we reached the door she said "Lets go and buy a cake at Mr. White's." Now, his baker's shop was in Milford Street, in exactly the opposite direction to school. In the shop we went (it always had a delicious smell of fresh baking) and Mum bought me an Easter Cake, bright yellow with scalloped edges and a cherry in the centre. I came out munching my prize and was so intent on eating that I didn't realise we had walked up Milford Hill, along Rampart Road, across into Saint Martin's Church Street and were outside the School. In I went with no more trouble. I don't think that I've been conned many times in my life, but without doubt this was one.

Just after this episode came "Black Tuesday", the day that I was sent home in disgrace. It happened that just before playtime my stomach ached. Too frightened to ask if I could please go to the lavatory (I was only three!) I hung on hoping that the bell would go for the mid-morning break. It didn't, but I did. I just sat there in my dirty trousers, hoping against hope that no-one would notice. The smell gave me away, for it was not long before Miss Hale said, "Who's been a dirty child". Then she went round the class, nose in air sniffing away and stopped near me. By this time my face as much as the smell probably gave me away. "Arthur Maidment — it's you". Oh the shame of it for she then went into the top class and fetched a big girl, Winnie Sanger, who lived in Milford Hill — she must have been all of six, to escort me home. A most humiliated small boy then had a most uncomfortable walk with the prospect of telling Mum what had happened. By the time that I reached home I expect the smell told my mother the sad story.

We sat at tiny desks of yellow wood with matching tiny carver chairs. When we learned to write, we started with sand-trays, tracing the letters in the sand with the forefinger on the right hand. Writing with the left was not allowed and it amazes me how many left-handed writers exist today. From sand-trays, we progressed to slates, framed in wood, writing with slate pencils which allowed the slates to be cleaned off after every lesson before being put away. After the slates, came green lino printed with red lines and on these we wrote with white chalk. The smell of this new lino is still a pleasant memory.

We had to learn to count with the help of a bead frame or abacus, which stood on legs at the front of the class. Thanks to Mum, however, I was proficient before I went to school. She had also ensured that I could manage simple reading and of course it was an advantage that I had two elder sisters who spent a deal of time teaching me. It must be much harder for the only or elder child, because so much can be taught by elder brothers or sisters. Perhaps taught is the wrong word as the knowledge is just acquired.

Soon after my third birthday, on which I had been given a rubber ball, I insisted against Mum's wishes in taking it to school. This ball was a beauty — brightly coloured — it had scenes from capitals around the world printed on it. I remember "The Eiffel Tower" and "The Statue of Liberty". I was so proud of that ball which must have been about three inches in diameter. That afternoon I left it in my coat in the lobby; when I went to get my coat after school, the ball had vanished and I cried and cried. When my sister came to fetch me, she calmed me down enough for me to explain what had happened and then took me to see Miss Hale, the Headmistress. Next day, the thief was asked to own up, but of course no-one did and so one more of life's lessons was learned the hard way — never be too trusting.

When in the Infants' School we used to spend a lot of time playing games like "Wallflowers" and "Ring-a-ring of roses". Later we graduated to dances like "Sir Roger de Coverley" and "The Lancers". I suppose this sort of thing kept the girls happy but we boys found our happiness each playtime, in the very early days playing railway engines. Four or five of us would go around the playground in file, left arms pumping round with elbows bent, the right arm outstretched touching the boy in front, all loudly puffing away. From about the age of six we progressed from this somewhat babyish game for we were now hooked on football. It has been my lifelong passion. During each break, providing it was fine, out came a tennis ball and we formed two teams — "Saint Martin's" and "Britford". Why Britford? I've no idea but I do remember that no-one wanted to play for Britford. The games were played very seriously and occasionally fights broke out — something small boys have been doing for a long long time.

One dinner time in 1920, Mum told me that the following day would be Dad's Birthday and that all the church bells would ring.

Naturally, I went back to school and broadcast the news, whereupon my friends branded me as a purveyor of untruths or words to that effect. The next day, I had the last laugh and felt like a conjuror who has pulled a rabbit from a hat, when the eight bells of St. Martin's Church started one of their marathon peals of umpteen hundred Grandshire Triples, for which the ringers were famed. Later that day I came back to earth when I learned that June 23rd was also The Prince of Wales' Birthday and that my Dad was not quite as famous as I had thought.

I remember one of the first reading books. It was a real shocker and used in schools for many years, dating back I believe to the middle of the last century. Called "Tommy Suck-a-Thumb", it had lurid illustrations of a very tall man chasing very small children. In his right hand was a pair of giant scissors, open at the ready to cut off the thumb of any child he saw sucking it. Undoubtedly the aim of the book was to stop thumb sucking but what a way to do it! Whenever I saw a tall man approaching, I looked to see if he had a pair of scissors with him. The book was the stuff of nightmares and I think my mother employed the best and quickest remedy — bitter aloes rubbed on the fingers and thumbs each night very quickly cures the habit.

When I was about six years of age, something which I learned at school came as a tremendous shock. It was on a Tuesday — another "black Tuesday". What was this piece of knowledge? It was nearing Christmas and one playtime I said to Alf Norris, my friend over many years, that I hoped Father Christmas would bring me a building set. He said, "Don't be daft, there's no Father Christmas — it's your Dad and Mum." Somehow I got through the rest of the morning in deepest gloom, rushed home to tell Mum, expecting to hear it wasn't true — instead my faith was finally shattered. Another of life's lessons was learned — never believe all that you are told.

During my last year in the Infants, I remember arriving back at school on a Monday and a party of soldiers in uniform was outside the church. My friends were standing by the school door, the church bell was tolling. I asked what was happening — "Is it a funeral?" — "Yes, Frank Cox's dad." This was a great shock for Frank was a classmate. His father had died as a result of War Service and he was to be given a Military Funeral. We were all devastated, for although having two classmates, whose fathers had been killed during the war, this was the first time that the death of a parent had come so close.

In 1921, I had gone through a slight stammering phase, which was quickly cured, thanks to Miss Rowden, an excellent teacher. However, when the School Christmas Play came along and I was cast as the fourth dwarf in "Snow White and the Seven Dwarfs", a problem arose. We rehearsed on Saturday afternoons and each week I stumbled over one line. I had to say, "Someone has been using my serviette", and just could not say serviette fluently. The big day was fast approaching and I dreaded making a mess of the line at the actual performance. Then fate took a hand for the father of Ken White, who was playing the first dwarf, was found dead as the result of a heart attack, on the kitchen floor of their Polden Road home, some ten days prior to the concert. Ken couldn't take his part, there was a reshuffle and I found myself as first dwarf. I had much more to say but didn't mind one little bit as it meant that I was excused from saying that word "serviette". To this day I still have pangs of guilt over my relief, when really I should have been feeling sorry for the White family and Ken in particular. He stayed on with his mother, but unfortunately his two elder brothers had to go away to Bristol and spent the next six years in a Salvation Army Home.

Something which pleased me at the end of that Christmas, 1921, was the retirement of The Headmistress, Miss Hale, who left to get married. She had always seemed very strict although, looking back, I have to admit that she was a good teacher. Her successor, Mrs. Stoakes was a middle-aged widow with three teenaged children and had a much greater understanding of small kiddies. Although she only taught me for one term, it was a happy time and I have memories of a very kindly lady.

Just before leaving the Infants School in the Spring of 1922, I arrived back after dinner to find my friends standing near the entrance to Saint Martin's Lane which led to the main Southampton Road (now Tollgate Road). Told that there had been an accident at the top of the lane, Alf Norris, John Tiller and I, made our way to the main road to find that there had indeed been an accident — a fatal one. Arthur Charlton, who had only left school the previous Easter, lived in Waterloo Gardens and was employed at Milford Railway Goods Station. Each day, one of the drivers at Pratts Petroleum Depot in Waterloo Road gave Arthur a lift back to work. It was his habit to slow down opposite the Station entrance to enable his unofficial passenger to jump off. Unfortunately on this day, Arthur slipped under the lorry and the solid tyred rear wheel passed over him, killing him instantly. When we arrived on the scene, all that remained to be seen was a very large pool of blood. We stood gazing at this in horror until some railwaymen on the other side of the road noticed us and we were told to b—— off, which we quickly did and ran all the way back to school. This was a tragic occurrence for Arthur was the only son of elderly parents, his father being a disabled clockmaker who was often unable to work.

3 The Boys' School

Monday week after Easter, 1922, saw a new and somewhat awesome change in my life. On Maundy Thursday, I had ceased to be a member of the top class Infants and now entered the Boys School, which at that time catered for seven to fourteen year olds — the latter being school leaving age. It was next door to the Infants School but we had heard terrifying stories about life there.

For starters the cane was used — apparently for the slightest misdemeanor. Not true: if you got the cane, generally it was well deserved. Boys were always bullied by those older and bigger. There was some truth in this but I expect the practice still goes on today. In my time though, it was largely checked by the monitors from Standard Seven — those near god-like boys who almost seemed like men.

We had also heard frightening stories about the teachers but with one exception I always found them very fair. If you stepped out of line, then look out, but you quickly learned to do as you were told at the greatest possible speed.

On the first morning came two shocks — I found that Christian names were dropped — from now on I was Maidment. Nicknames are a favourite pastime with small boys and so during the next four years and one term I was known to my school mates as "Pavement". The second shock was when the biggest boy in the class - he was nearly a head taller than me and considerably heavier — Jack Truckle would not stop talking. After several warnings he was called to the front of the class, told to hold out his hand and caned by Miss Smith with the flat of a foot ruler. This caning had its effect for the whole class knew that Miss Smith would stand no nonsense and it stamped her authority.

I believe that at this time St. Martin's Boys School offered a good education within the financial limits available. The Headmaster, Mr. E.J. Russ had himself been taught at the school in the eighteen-nineties

Mr. Ernest Russ, Headmaster of St. Martin's Boys' School — a wonderful teacher, kindly, but a strict disciplinarian.

— my father had been one of his contemporaries. He rode to school on one of the high "sit up and beg" bikes with a saddle on the crossbar, which enabled him to take his daughter from his home at Harnham to school at The Godolphin. He had a peculiar way of dismounting — instead of putting his right leg over the saddle in the usual fashion, he used to put his left leg on a step protruding from the rear spindle, stand on this and gently place his right leg to the ground.

Mr. Russ was an excellent teacher — a fair man, but whilst a strict disciplinarian, was kindly. Not only did he make sure that we had a thorough grounding in the 3 Rs, Reading — Writing — Rithmatic, but just as important — he taught us C. P. and K. — Courtesy, Politeness and Kindness:

"If you meet a lady, she may be a Duchess or a lady tramp, you raise your cap." "When walking with a lady always walk on the outside of the pavement."

"Should you see a lady that you know, carrying a basket, and you are going in the same direction, offer to carry it for her."

These lessons were given at the right time and were invaluable in later life.

On Sunday afternoons, Mr. Russ took the Church Sunday School and he would not brook any boy not attending either his or some other Sunday School of another denomination. Occasionally he would come into the classroom during the week and say,

"Hand up anyone who did not attend a Sunday School last Sunday."

No-one dared to lie and those admitting to the lapse were told,

"If you don't belong to any Sunday School you will be at mine next Sunday".

In those days parents did not complain at such authoritarian behaviour — they knew better than argue with Mr. Russ who was a greatly respected member of the community.

I remember one Monday morning, just after we went into the Boys' School, he came into Standard One and brought with him, from our class, Jim Weeks, who had been absent when the registers were called. The headmaster stood at the front of the class with Jim looking rather embarrassed and announced,

"Weeks has been before the magistrates this morning and has been discharged without a stain on his character. If any boy says anything to Weeks about it I will cane him."

No-one knew that Jim was even in trouble and to this day I don't know what it was all about. This happened in the days before Juvenile Courts and it must have been a terrifying experience to be taken into the Court as a seven-year-old to be tried.

Mr. Russ's deputy was Mr. Windust, then probably in his late thirties — always smart and well turned out. A keen sportsman, he was one of the mainstays of St. Martin's Cricket Club in the Salisbury and District League where his really fast bowling was feared by opponents. He also played football for Salisbury Corinthians. Not for nothing was he known as Windy — when upset he really did "blow his top" but his bark was worse than his bite — he was an excellent teacher and took both Standards Six and Seven. Under his leadership the School won the local Schools Leagues in Football, Cricket and Swimming. "Windy" went on to become Headmaster of a School in Weymouth.

The Standard Five master Sammy Edwards was a quite volatile character much given to boxing his pupils ears — not only a painful but also dangerous practice. It was said in his defence that he had been through a tough war as an Infantry NCO and the award of the Military Medal was proof of his bravery. Despite or maybe because of his frequent outbursts he was a good teacher and got results. Eventually he became the school's headmaster but by that time his rather late marriage had somewhat tamed this fiery individual.

In contrast Ralph Shergold who took Standard Four was not only a splendid teacher but also one of the nicest men I have ever known. He stood some six feet four inches tall and was so big as a young teenager, that playing as a goalkeeper for the Bishop Wordsworth's School against Osborne House School at Romsey he was unable to stand under the six-foot goalposts. Ralph made a friend of every pupil and on their birthday they were called to his desk and presented with a sixpence — quite a lot of money in the twenties. I am pleased to say that later in life, Ralph and I became very close friends. A wonderful man and a fine teacher.

Mr. Smith, the Standard Three master was at this time nearing retirement. A homely man of stocky build he sported an untidy moustache. He too was kind but stood no nonsense and had no problems with discipline. Each morning he came in from his Alderbury home on a belt-driven Douglas motor bike with sidecar. Even during the summer term he was wrapped up against the elements in waterproof jacket and leggings — his head encased in a leather helmet with ear-flaps. There was never a shortage of helpers to lift the bike up on to the pavement — over the school step and into the passage. I expect he could have managed the operation much more easily by himself.

Standard Two was under the control of Miss Judd, a very nice lady whose home was at Winterslow, where she returned in 1924 as Headmistress. She never used the cane but was one of the finest teachers I have known. If only she was alive today to pass on the secrets of her success.

The bottom class — Standard One was taught by Miss Smith (no relation to the Standard Three Master). A short, dumpy lady shaped rather like a cottage loaf, she seldom smiled and woe betide anyone not paying attention. One of her missions in life was to try and instil an Oxford accent into small boys who had a pronounced Wiltshire one. I am afraid that she had no success with me but I remember our chanting of "Rowned and rowned — up and dowwnn — rowned and rowned." Like all the members of staff, Miss Smith was dedicated to her work and she gave us a fine start in life.

The door to the school was in St. Martin's, Church Street, on the right hand side of the two storey building. It opened onto a six foot wide passage, on the left hand side of which was the rear wall of Standard Two. At the end of this wall leading off to the left was another passage to the downstairs lobby and the stairway to the first floor. The main passage led through to the playground via three brick steps and a slope. The toilets and urinals were to the left of this section — the urinals being roofless and thus open to the elements.

Standards One and Two were taught on the ground floor — a large room divided by sliding screens. Each section was supposed to be heated by a coke fired tortoise stove and large hot water pipes but in mid-winter it was really cold unless you were lucky enough to sit near the fire. Both classes shared a lobby which had racks on two levels for coats. Lobbies were unheated and so if you hung your coat up wet then wet it stayed. There were never enough hooks so each one had to take several coats. There were four cracked wash basins, never any soap and one roller towel, changed on Friday afternoons, by which time it was not only dirty but had a horrible smell.

The stairs had metal caps to prevent wear so the noise from

marching feet was horrendous, most boys did nothing to lessen the din, in fact a favourite ploy was to stamp the right foot down hard in unison. The clatter was quite effective until one of the masters stamped down on the offenders. The stairway went up ten stairs to a landing with a large window, then up another ten to the first floor. To the left of this was the Headmaster's room. In front, Standard Three a small classroom and to the right a glass panelled door leading to another large room, similar to the one downstairs and again divided by sliding screens. In the first section, Standards Six and Seven were taught, the latter in a corner alcove, usually consisting of about twelve to fourteen boys. On the far side of the screen was Standard Four, whilst through a door at the back right hand side of this room was Standard Five. This was by far the most pleasant room in the school for it backed onto St. Martin's Church and in the far left hand corner was a door, normally open during the summer, leading to the fire escape.

The playground was on two levels, the top one quite small and asphalted — for use only by Standard Seven. The lower — rough gravel and during the winter months flooded at the far end. The whole playground was surrounded by a four foot high brick wall with buttresses at about every ten feet. These provided a source of torture. If you were put on the rack, you were pinned with your back to the buttress — two boys, one on each side took your arms, put one foot up on the edge of the buttress and pulled — it was painful. I have often wondered if the torture I suffered left permanent damage for although only 5' 10" in height, my reach is 6' 3". The rule of thumb is that height equals reach. Perhaps I was stretched on the rack.

When you arrived in the Boys' School, you quickly learned the rules. As at all schools a playground full of youngsters was bedlam. However, by means of a whistle, order was swiftly obtained from chaos. One long blast on the whistle from Mr. Windust and everyone came to attention on the spot with not a sound to be heard. Then a short blast and six monitors took up position at the top of the lower playground. Now two short blasts and the school lined up in twos behind the monitors — Standard One on the left — Six to the right. Another short blast and the school moved off to the various classrooms. Any talking in lines brought swift retribution. The only exception to this procedure was on those days that we went to a service in the church. On these occasions, Standard One lined up in single file whilst Standard Six would line up

Standard 2 at St. Martin's Boys' in 1923:
Back Row: *Stickland, Cox, Malcolm, Fulford, Hart, Short, Chorley, Watts, Musselwhite, Pearce;*
Centre Row: *Haskell, Maidment, Whitmarsh, Lodge, Tiller, Norris, True, Day, Weeks, Goodfellow;*
Front Row: *Muspratt, Read, Cook, Whitehorn, Macey, White, Truckle.*

beside them. This meant that each small boy was accompanied to church by an older boy whose job it was to find the hymns and generally ensure good behaviour.

We used to return to school at half-past one in the afternoons and precisely at 1.32p.m. Mr. Russ would take up position just inside the street door armed with his cane. Those unfortunates who were late received two cuts from the weapon - one on each hand and were admonished not to be late again. A friend of mine, who unfortunately was killed on a bombing mission over Germany in 1942 was always late — he never learned. However the message soon got home to me so that today, nearly seventy years on, I always make a point of being early.

After the latecomers had been dealt with, the Headmaster commenced his tour of inspection, starting with Standard Two. Standard One was excused this ritual. Still armed with the cane he would sweep into the classroom and say "Hands show". You raised your hands, palms to the front, shoulder high. If they were grubby, you were told to put your hand out and you had a cut with cane, a punishment which was then meted out to the other hand, followed by the order — "Go and wash". It was hard — might possibly have been cruel but with most pupils it worked. Unless you were very dim you quickly learned to be early and clean.

In the 'twenties playing hookey was almost unknown. Each week the City Attendance Officer called to check the registers for absentees. If no excuse had been sent he called on the parents, so truancy was kept to a minimum. The officer, Mr. Matthews, who lived in St. Ann's Street, was a keen member of the Local Amateur Dramatic Society and visited schools in another capacity — that of conjuror — an art in which he excelled.

On arrival in Standard One you started to learn your tables. I know that many teachers of the present day think that learning by rote is archaic. Nonsense — it is the quickest way to learn and, what is more, is never forgotten. In fact most children find it enjoyable to recite in unison, in sing song fashion:-

One one is one
Two ones are two
Three ones are three,
and so on

We also had to learn a great deal of poetry by heart - poetry which I can still recall all these years later.

By the time that you were ready to go up into Standard Three, you had to be proficient to the twelve times table but it did not stop there for later on you had measurement, area, weight and many others. One which I found to be of great value in my business life, until the advent of decimalisation, was learnt in Standard Four, in the usual sing-song fashion. It went:-

Of one pound 10/- a half 6/8 a third
5/- a quarter 4/- a fifth 2/6 an eighth
2/- a tenth 1/4 a fifteenth 1/3 a sixteenth
1/- a twentieth 6d a fortieth and 3d an eightieth

Once you learnt in this way it was easily recalled.

One of the big changes we had to cope with, was learning to write with pen and ink. The pens had the ordinary steel nibs and it was essential that they had just the right amount of ink on them or blots resulted. Then again, the pen had to be held at an exact angle and Miss Smith had her own very efficient method of quickly teaching this. She would patrol the class, a wooden foot ruler at the ready in her hand, if she saw you holding the pen incorrectly, down came the ruler on your knuckles. We sat at long desks which held five pupils. Inkwells were let into the top of the desks and each Friday afternoon the ink monitors from Standard Seven would arrive with trays, collect these inkwells, take them into the lobby and refill them with very watery ink from a small water can. Our pens were collected up at the end of each session, so we never got the same pen twice, resulting in the nibs being frequently crossed. After a few weeks most boys bought their own pens and they were usually carried down the top of the right sock.

The socks of the twenties were of the turnover top variety — the tops usually being brightly striped. Uniforms were unknown in elementary schools, in fact it is difficult to describe the varied attire. Quite a number of boys had "hand-me-downs" previously worn by elder brothers. Often these garments were too big and it was quite common to see a jersey being made a better fit with the aid of a large safety pin. Some boys wore boots which had not only had previous owners and were not well fitting but also had soles and heels covered with metal studs. These cost only fourpence a pound and no doubt were a good means to provide longer life to footwear. The wearers of boots shod in this way came into their own during icy weather when they were able to outslide everyone else.

We were all expected to work hard and at the end of each term we had examinations. The total marks which could be awarded for the combined subjects was 100. On the last day of term the school assembled in the large upstairs room which had the screens pulled back for the occasion. Starting with Miss Smith for Standard One, the teachers would go to the Headmaster's desk on the dais and read the complete class results. Then Mr. Russ would call the names of the top boys who went up to receive a silver threepenny piece. Next they had to face the assembled school and were given three cheers. The competition engendered was very keen. I see nothing wrong in competition at an early age because it prepares you for later life when everyone has to face it.

An early major event in my life in the Boys' School was the celebration of Empire Day on May 24th, which has now been renamed Commonwealth Day. For this Annual Event wooden forms were taken out into St. Martin's Church Street and men used to manhandle the piano down the stairs to take it outside. It never seemed to rain on Empire Day. On the opposite side of the road from the school was the Rectory Wall some fifteen feet in height, massively constructed of large flints. The whole school would be assembled in the street, Mr. Windust being in charge, whilst the official party sat in the Rectory Garden, just behind the top of the wall on which was draped a huge Union Jack.

I remember many of those in the official party:- The Rector, Reverend Ian Grant Cameron, The Curate, Reverend Arthur Reeves who was a Newfoundlander, Major General Sir Henry Everett and Lady Everett who lived at Avon Turn, Alderbury. Brigadier and Mrs. Carter lived in a large house in Brown Street — he was fat, very pompous with a waxed moustache, having exceptionally long spikes; Major Forbes from Fowlers Hill, who not only looked like but also dressed like King George V — whether by accident or design I don't know, Mrs. Bowyer, the widow of an Australian Bishop who lived in Fowlers Road was very big and wore outsize hats which accentuated her size and finally the Headmaster, Mr. E.J. Russ.

At a signal we stood, made a right turn and faced the church where the verger waited to unfurl the flag of St. George. We then sang The National Anthem and Mr. Russ addressed us on the subject of patriotism. Boys from the top class read poems by Rudyard Kipling and Sir Henry Newbolt interspersed with the singing of such patriotic songs as "Land of Hope and Glory", "Hearts of Oak", "A wet sheet and a flowing sea" and others of this nature. The final song still is vividly in my memory:-

The British Flag is never furled,
It greets its sons and daughters,
Along the highways round the world,
Above its winding waters,
It speaks of their dear motherland,

And tells her tale of glory,
For all her children, hand in hand
Must carry on that story.

Then came the chorus:-

It stands as it has always stood,
For honour, duty, brotherhood,
For God and King and Right,
For we shall live and we shall die,
That evermore our flag shall fly,
For God and King and Right.

That summer of 1922 was extremely hot and dry. Mr. Russ must have been a bit of a psychologist as he had us singing "Summer Suns are glowing" quite often at morning assembly. He seemed to choose hymns that suited the weather. The sun took its toll in August when I went to Britford Sheep Fair with my Uncle Arthur, a civil servant who used to have the whole month for holiday and returned home to learn that Ron Stanley, a schoolmate who lived in The Friary, had died from sunstroke. This was the only time that I can remember such a fatality occurring locally during my lifetime. For the rest of the summer no children were allowed out without wearing hats.

Just after my birthday in September 1922, we came out from afternoon school on a Tuesday and, on reaching the corner of St. Martin's Church Street, saw quite a lot of people at the bottom of St. Ann's Street. Apparently Mr. Dolman had been working at The Albion Hotel, fell from a very tall ladder and was killed. Mrs. Dolman was well known to Mum through the Mothers' Union, the only son Roger was a Standard Seven boy and he had four younger sisters including one who was about a year old. I remember being glad that my father had a job which did not need him to climb ladders. Mrs. Dolman was even shorter than my mother's — 4' 10", but she did a wonderful job in bringing up her family single handed after the tragic death of her husband.

Toward the end of the year, we were given a holiday on a Thursday because the school was being used as a polling station for the General Election. Although we were only in Standard One, on the day prior to the holiday, Mr. Russ took the trouble to come to our class and explain how the election worked — how a vote was cast, placed in a sealed box, taken to the Council Chamber for counting and how the result was declared. He even brought one of the polling booths for us to examine. Until this time, politics had meant nothing to me. Now I learnt that whilst Mum was a lifelong Conservative, Dad was a determined Liberal, although neither shouted their allegiance. I heard my mother tell a friend that being a Liberal was Dad's only fault!

On the morning of the election the parties' colours, in the two horse race, were much in evidence. Conservative Blue and Red for Liberal. Even small boys sported rosettes and, as happens amongst youngsters, fights broke out. Early in the afternoon things began to hot up. Some of the drovers, usually employed in the Cattle Auction Marts, were well plied with beer and in no time were leading processions of small and

St. Ann's Street in the mid-twenties. Note the early Victorian gas lamp-standard on the left. These were only replaced in August 1939, one week before the arrival of the Second World War black-out.

some not so small children around the city, processions which seemed mainly to support the Conservative cause. Mr. Beauchamp (pronounced Beecham as in pills) was a well known procession leader. He was furnished with a big drum and plenty of liquid refreshment meant that before long he not so much marched as fell around the city. If you wanted to join in the fun, it was essential to find something to beat with a stick — an old tin tray, an empty box or tin, even a piece of plywood — the instruments were legion — no matter as long as they created noise. We lined up behind old "Beachie" as he was known and off we went around the City streets. Mum had no idea that I joined in. As we progressed we beat away then Beachie gave three quick beats on his drum, the noise stopped — and we sang the ditty:-

Vote, Vote, Vote for Mr. Morrison,
Kick Spencer Moulton out of town,
We'll buy a penny gun,
And we'll shoot him up the —,
Then he won't come to Salisbury any more.

No, the rude word was not sung at the end of the fourth line but the implication was there. It was good fun but thank goodness my parents never learned of my involvement. I don't suppose these efforts influenced the election in the slightest, but on the Friday we learned that Mr. Morrison had been re-elected and felt that we had done our part in ensuring his success.

On reaching my eighth birthday, I became eligible to join the Juvenile Section of The Salisbury Public Library, something which I quickly did. Over the next few years the Assistant Librarian, Miss Liddell, probably got fed up with the sight of me as I used to get through several books each week and must have read most of the stock. There were few new books added each year and I would think that a great number of volumes had been in the Library from its opening in 1905. I became hooked on adventure stories by R.L. Stevenson, Ballantyne, Rider Haggard and many more. Through their writings, I went in my imagination on trips to unknown parts — coral islands, hunting for treasure, discovering oil — joining the Library opened up an entirely new world for me.

The Annual Christmas Concert took place in the hall of the

Teachers' Training College at Barnards Cross. The building was part of the College at King's House in the Close but was used as living quarters by students of non-conformist persuasion. It was quite a large hall with a good stage. I remember quite a number of the items from my first Boys' School Concert, one was the carol, "Away in a Manger", sung by Henry Musselwhite. It was the first time I had heard it. The boys of Standard Seven did quite a clever act — there was a screen across the stage on which music had been painted — the notes were holes in the screen and the boys had their heads through these whilst in their mouths were small bazookas — small sound instruments. By careful timing they gave good renderings of a number of popular tunes. The evening ended with a Pirate Play and I went home thinking what a wonderful concert, as it probably was for an elementary school having no spare cash.

The following day was the end of term and I shall never forget the shock when Miss Smith read the Class Examination results for I thought my name would never come. The previous term I had been placed third — now my position was sixth. It was a great disappointment but I made up my mind there and then that it would be different next term. Right from the first day I worked hard, no longer rested on my oars and as a result topped the class list. The silver threepenny piece that I received as reward was hard earned but the episode taught me a lesson early in life — that good results are only achieved by extra effort.

4 *The street where I lived*

Salisbury had been laid out in the thirteenth century, rather in the fashion of the twentieth century garden cities. Houses were built at the street frontage, whilst the interiors of each square or chequer provided garden space. It was a wonderful vision but over the course of centuries, the gardens became building plots, access to the new houses being obtained by demolishing part of the ground floor of a house to provide a passageway through to the new dwellings. These back developments known as courts could be found in most of the older city streets of my boyhood. Thankfully they have now gone as they really were substandard. However, it is interesting to note that in a City History of 1830, reference is made to "the ideal dwellings for the working class now being erected by Mr. Penniston." The ideal dwellings of 1830 had become slums by 1920 for Penniston's Court in Culver Street consisted of twelve tiny houses, sharing a communal sink with two taps at the end of the courtyard and four communal toilets. How the quite respectable people who lived under these conditions managed to bring up families, I shall never know.

On the west side of Culver Street at the Milford Street junction was Jenkins' Shop, having a window in each street with the door across the corner. It was not large but did a fairish trade. Noted for its cleanliness, it was owned by Mrs. Jenkins, although the work was done by her daughter and son-in-law, Mr. & Mrs. Cecil Bevis. On entering the shop, facing you was a glass showcase with a marble top for the counter. Shelving covered the back two walls, whilst to the right was a biscuit stand containing some dozen tins, stacked at an angle so that by just taking off the lid, biscuits could be removed. Jenkins did quite a delivery trade, the goods being taken out by Mr. Bevis on a very old "errand boy's" bike with a wicker basket at the front. They used to sell cut-corned beef at 2d a quarter pound, broken biscuits for 6d a pound,

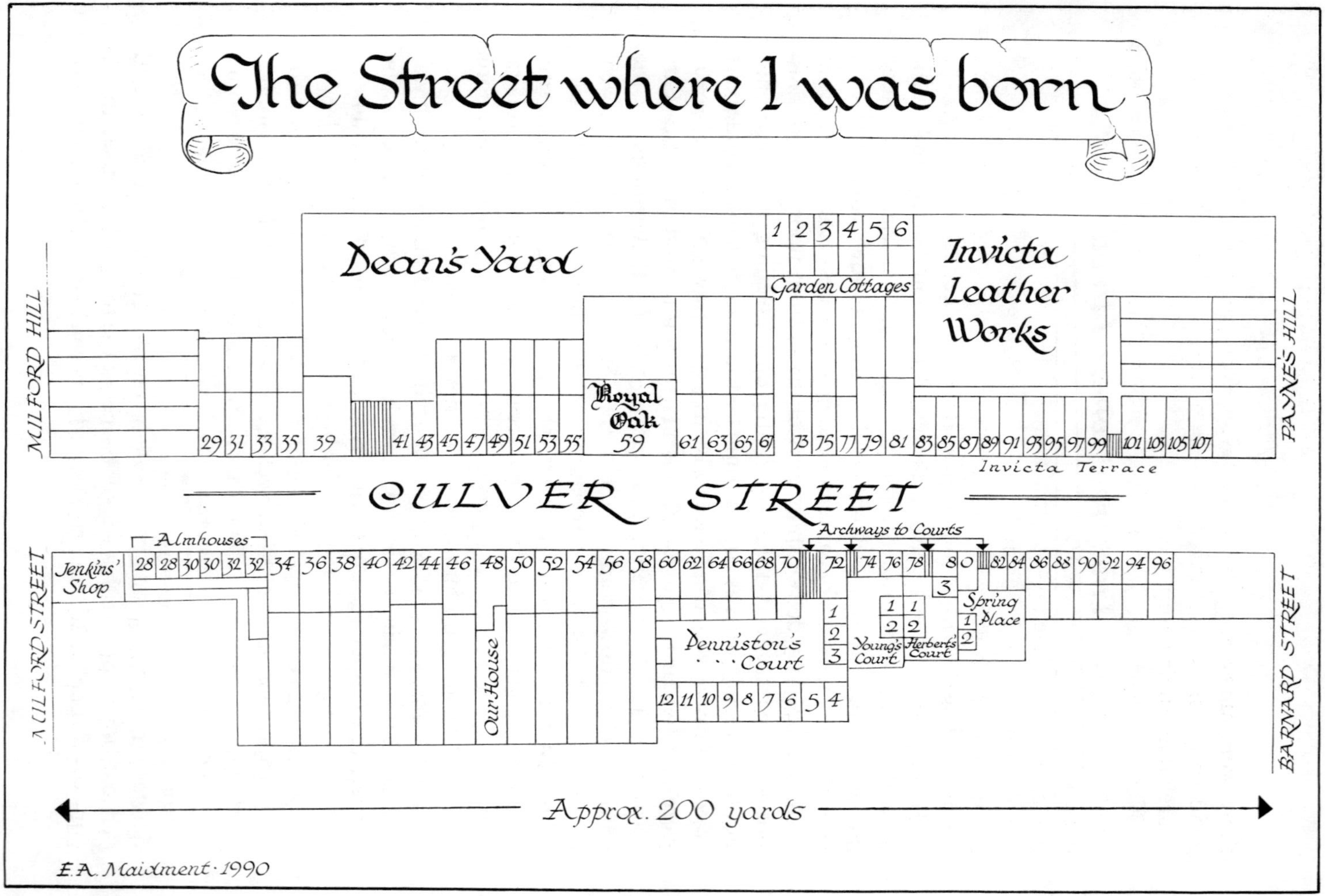
The Street where I was born
Dean's Yard
Garden Cottages
Invicta Leather Works
Royal Oak
59
Invicta Terrace
MILFORD HILL
PAYNE'S HILL
CULVER STREET
Archways to Courts
Almhouses
Jenkins' Shop
Our House
Denniston's Court
Young's Court
Herbert's Court
Spring Place
MILFORD STREET
BARNARD STREET
Approx. 200 yards
E.A. Maidment · 1990

there were many of these in the days before packaging. It was not a good shop for sweets, the ones which were stocked always seemed dearer than their competitors.

Next to the shop in Culver Street were six Church almshouses which had been rebuilt in the eighteen-forties to replace the original dwellings. Each pair of houses shared a front door, staircase and a passageway which led to the small rear yard. They had a tiny room on the ground floor lit by a small leaded window and heated by an open fire from which as much smoke seemed to blow into the room as went up the chimney. The almshouses' occupants were old ladies who, to be eligible, had to be of good character and lifelong churchwomen. Not only did they live rent free but also received 3/6 per week. The last of the six was occupied by Miss Kate Grace, a cripple from birth, who spent almost all day and every day standing on her crutches at the street door. She was thus well informed of the movements of her neighbours and managed to find out any gossip that was going. As she was not in receipt of Old Age Pension, she was a lot younger than the other ladies, her church allowance was 4/- per week. I remember the amounts because for several years, it was my Saturday job to go to St. Martin's Church Vestry to collect the money which was paid out by the Parish Clerk, Mr. Daniel Sutton, who before retirement had been Headmaster of the Church School. He would sit at the head of the long table, the various amounts were packed in white paper with the name of the recipient on each. As you collected each one, you read out the name and amount — if it was 3/6 you had to say three shillings and sixpence — no short cuts for Daniel — then sign for the money in the large Parish Account Book. I remember one list — having read it so often:-

Mrs. Cassey	*Three Shillings and Sixpence*
Mrs. Yeates	*Three Shillings and Sixpence*
Mrs. Dew	*Three Shillings and Sixpence*
Mrs. Mullins	*Three Shillings and Sixpence*
Mrs. Norris	*Three Shillings and Sixpence*
Miss Grace	*Four Shillings*

Mr. Sutton was a nice old gentleman — looked distinguished with his white hair and small white beard, a stickler for accuracy and forever telling me that my father had been one of his pupils.

The houses next to these almshouses were quite modern for the street — probably having been built in the eighteen-seventies. They formed a terrace of four and the front doors opened onto a passage whereas most houses had the door opening directly into a room. I remember the occupants: the Barretts, the Reeves, the Penneys and the Sangers. Mr. Barrett worked in the Town Yard, Mr. Reeves was a jobbing gardener whilst Mr. Sanger, who was a poulterer, was always in demand each Christmas when the chicken which so many residents kept were due to be plucked and prepared for the table. They always seemed to smell of singed feathers when they came back.

Next came Mrs. Sutton's shop — very old and very small — a two storey building with a roof of lovely weathered tiles. This must have started life as a cottage — the front room which had been turned into the shop was only about ten feet by eight feet. The door, a long way from being square, was at the left of the shop window and on entering you had the impression of walking downhill. On the right was the counter behind which, flanked by shelving was a blocked-up chimney breast. Near the window was a small pair of scales with polished brass weights whilst at the other end of the counter was a larger pair with iron weights used for the vegetables which were kept in the left hand corner of the shop. The window was crammed with sweets in boxes and glass jars and she kept an amazing selection. Quite a number of things could be bought for a halfpenny — Barretts Sherbet Fountains with liquorice straws, Sherbet Dabs with their lump of toffee on a stick, Liquorice Ropes, Humbugs, Spearmint Lumps, Aniseed Balls were 20 for a penny. Mrs Sutton sold all sorts of items not only tea, sugar, butter and other essentials but also innumerable medicines, corn cures, pot menders and suchlike, all displayed on hanging cards at the back of the shop. Beechams Pills could be bought one at a time in a spill for a penny. I wonder what happened to Seidlitz Powders. Presumably they went out of favour because when one thinks about them, they must have been dangerous. If you had a stomach upset you were sent to Mrs. Sutton who sold you a powder for tuppence. The packet contained two smaller packets — one blue, one white, which were mixed together in a tumbler of water. The mixture fizzed like mad, you swallowed the concoction and with little delay sprinted for the nearest lavatory, hoping that your speed would be faster than the deadly powder.

The house next to Mrs. Sutton's was of about the same age but as the pavement was almost a foot higher than the floor of the front room, it had two steps down inside the door. This applied to many houses in the street, presumably brought about by the making up of the road with gravel over a long period. As the road became higher the house levels were left behind. This tiny cottage was occupied by a charming, grandmotherly lady called Mrs. Newman.

Now came five tall three storey houses belonging to St. Martin's Church and, although making a terrace, each was slightly different to its neighbour. The properties had been left to the Church in the early eighteenth century and were let at moderate rents. I would imagine that the site had at one time been occupied by a large merchant's house as four of the houses were built over a medieval cellar. This had a separate entrance and had been used for many purposes — the storage of deeds by the Wilts and Dorset Bank, prior to this by Mr. Pern, a solicitor, but when I was a small boy it had been leased to The Haunch of Venison Inn as a wine store and bottling plant.

Each house had two rooms and scullery on the ground floor and two bedrooms on each of the upper storeys. The first, no. 46, was occupied in 1914 by Inspector Ainsworth of the City Police Force. On his departure the following year his two neighbours in nos. 48 and 50 moved along — Mrs. Jeffery taking no. 46 and Mrs. Tapper (my grandmother) no. 48. I cannot remember Mrs. Jeffery who must have died when I was quite small but her two daughters Miss Lottie Jeffery, a cripple and Mrs. Bruton continued living in the house. The latter had been widowed very early in life — her husband Ernest, a member of a footballing family had played for Salisbury City, then Southampton as a professional goalkeeper. After playing in a match during a snowstorm he caught pneumonia which led to fatal tuberculosis. Their only daughter Olive followed her father to an early grave as the result of the same complaint which was such a terrible scourge during the years prior to the Second World War. Between their house and ours were the double doors of the cellar, having a three inch steel bar which fitted over a staple and was fastened by an enormous padlock. Number 50 was the home of the Bannell family — father, mother and two daughters — one of whom was deformed and made a living, hand-weeding the lawns in The Close, one son a tailor, who was a cripple and one granddaughter. After visiting the Public Houses, father and son could become quite violent with one another and I can remember the noisy encounters they had. The next house had been occupied by the Dear Family for several generations. Living there were Mrs. Dear, her elder daughter, another daughter with her husband who was a main line engine driver and their three children. When they finally moved out their successors found the floor covered with six layers of linoleum — the bottom ones must have been in position for many a long year!

At no. 52 lived Mr. Maton with his elderly spinster sister, a very quiet couple whose family had been in the house for almost two centuries. Miss Maton died in 1923 and about a year later I remember that my friends and I were playing in the street when there was a sudden shout from a young man. Mr. Maton had worked for many years as a solicitor's clerk, he had not turned up for work that day, the young man sent to check the reason had found Mr. Maton dead in the kitchen, the small loaf collected on his way home from work the previous evening still in its wrapping on the table. He had died from natural causes.

Next to the Matons came two small two storey houses also in the ownership of the church. The first was occupied by Miss Trimby, the last of a family that had lived there for a long time whilst her neighbours were Mr. & Mrs. Collins with their middle-aged bachelor son.

Then came five small cottages, each having matchboard front doors with the old-fashioned push-down type of latch. Just inside the door were two steps down to a small living room about ten feet square, behind this was a tiny scullery and the houses had two small bedrooms upstairs. At the rear was a minute yard with lavatory. I remember these houses well, because in the first lived two school-friends, Ron and Reg Bruton. Their father was a cabman and spent most of his time waiting for fares outside the Railway Station, the horse-drawn cabs being owned by Ivamy's of Milford Street. Their neighbours were the Grants, a quiet family. Continuing on down the street the Ahearns, a Catholic family who were all of small stature, the Frys, another quiet family and the Vincents who in contrast to the Ahearns were all well built — in fact the sons could all have made good guardsmen.

Mrs. Burden who lived at number 70, another two storey house was quite a character. She spent every fine day sitting in a chair just outside her front door. Her booming voice, very frightening to children, was usually occupied in gossiping to every passer-by. I have seen many cartoons of American grandmothers in rocking chairs on their front porches and am always reminded of Mrs. Burden, although she never had a clay pipe in her mouth.

The entrance to Pennistons Court was through an opening between the Burdens and the next cottage which was occupied by the Stanford family — the court entrance being under some of Burden's bedrooms. In the court were twelve tiny cottages and I only remember a few of the families who were unfortunate enough to live there — the Pragnells, Goodfellows, Wheadons, Dears, Rattues and Dawkins. Next to the Stanfords was Youngs Court — two exceptionally small dark cottages — again Church property — occupied by two maiden ladies — Miss Young and Miss Thomas. The rent was one shilling and tenpence for each dwelling — I remember the amount because Miss Young went to the Church Vestry to pay for both herself and her neighbour each Saturday morning at the same time that I was collecting the pensions for the Almshouse Ladies. She was very genteel, softly spoken and, although poor, kept standards high — her gloves, although well mended were always beautifully white. On the other side of the court entrance were three narrow two storey houses, each having a frontage of no more than eight feet. Then came another court — "Herberts", the entrance to the two houses was no more than three feet in width. They were very small, one up one down, their front doors opening into this narrow courtyard. As the sun could never shine into the houses at any time of the day they must have been cold and damp.

Next to the court was Mr. Stone's Grocery Shop which never seemed to do much trade — it opened late and closed early — the stock was limited so few people patronised it. Mr. Stone was an old man with a full white beard although he had a daughter several years younger than me.

On the other side of the shop was Spring Place — a misnomer if ever there was one. It was similar to Herberts Court and, although containing three houses, had the same drawbacks. To live in these courts must have been like living in perpetual gloom, thank goodness they were some of the first to go during the rehousing purge between the wars.

By the entrance to Spring Place were two two-storey houses the first occupied by the Henstridge family, then followed a terrace of six, gaunt looking three-storey houses built from a singularly unattractive deep red brick. They had no gardens but only tiny yards to the rear. In the first of these, number 86, lived a school friend Frank Gurd, and I also remember the Griggs, the Emm, the Trowbridge and the Marsh families. In about 1923 the eldest Marsh girl joined the chorus of one of the variety shows playing at the Palace Theatre and went on tour. She was probably about twenty at the time and on her return created quite a furore among the ladies with her hair shingled in the latest fashion and sporting lipstick and rouge which was almost unknown at that period.

Right at the end of the street was the wall of a very old building, the entrance being around the corner in Barnards Cross. This was used as a bacon store by Sainsbury's, grocery wholesalers whose main warehouse was behind The Crystal Fountain in Milford Street and who ran a fleet of chain driven lorries. This store always looked most unhygenic and no doubt saw more than its fair share of rats.

On the corner of the opposite side was a house which had seen far better days but thankfully has now been restored. The entrance was in Paynes Hill and doubtless this well designed building had started life as a Merchants house. It was occupied by the Fry family — the eldest son was Sergeant Major of St. Martin's Church Lads Brigade who used to camp out in bell tents at Shady Bower during the summer months. The house was bounded on its Culver Street frontage by Invicta Terrace — a row of thirteen identical dwellings having two rooms and a scullery downstairs and three bedrooms on the first floor, though none of the rooms were of any size. They did however have the convenience of a rear entrance. This was reached through a six-foot wide gateway with double doors which also served the houses in Paynes Hill.

In the first Invicta Terrace House, number 107, lived Mr. & Mrs. Sturgess with their son and daughter. Mrs. Sturgess was the hard working cleaner/caretaker of St. Martin's Boys' School whilst her husband worked in one of the many mineral water factories, unfortunately he had lost one eye in an industrial accident for which apparently no compensation was paid. Poor Mrs. Sturgess — she had to clean the school singlehanded, light the stoves, fill the scuttles, and the job was only part-time! How the poor lady must have worked. Other family names which come to mind as living in this terrace include Cobb, Welsh, Conduit, Weston, Andrews, Bannell and Godwin. Mr. Tom Andrews, whom I remember as a very old man, had worked at The White Hart Hotel and even in his old age was in demand if a ham had to be sliced for a wedding or similar function. To watch him was to see a master at work — each slice so thin and of unvarying thickness. His carving knife was only about half an inch wide at the centre where constant sharpening had worn it away.

A pair of semi-detached houses which seemed rather out of place adjoined Invicta Terrace. Much more modern than anything else in the street, they were well designed and built in glossy red brick. The Tanner and Dear families lived in them — Mr. Tanner was another engine driver whilst his neighbour Mr. Dear did upholstery. These beautiful three storey dwellings were next to three very poor looking, low two-storey cottages, in the first of which lived Mr. Clements with his family. He was a familiar face in the City as he cycled round each evening with his pole, lighting the gas lamps in the streets. He would reach up catch the chain on the left hand side with his hook — a quick pull — a plop and on came the light — and the poor chap had to circle the city again in the morning and pull down the right hand side to extinguish them. In between times during the day he had to take a short ladder, laid across the bike and make sure the lamps were clean. Next to the Clements were the Slark family, then the Burtons, after which came the entrance to Garden Cottages. Funny thing was they had no gardens and were built right up against the old City Rampart. They were quite tiny houses having no convenience and were reputed to be very damp.

On the other side of the entrance to Garden Cottages was a small house in the occupation of Mr. Truckle who was a coalman and his wife who worked for many years at The Salisbury Steam Laundry. She was a busy little woman, who scuttled everywhere, her feet hardly seeming to touch the ground. Next came a terrace of three three-storey houses, in the first lived the Salisburys, the name always amused me when I was small. Mr. Salisbury was a bootmaker. In the middle house were Mrs. Cotton and her middle-aged son Fred who was, to use a Wiltshire expression, "a bit light in the top storey." He did all sorts of odd jobs to earn a living. In the next house, Miss Goulding seemed to toil from morning to night at top speed to ensure that the laundry she worked on was ready dor delivery by Fred Cotton. Her work was a credit to her, for in those days, long before washing machines and tumble driers she would wash, dry and iron sheets for the princely sum of 4d. Somehow she made a living. Mr. and Mrs. Fairchild kept the pub next door —

The Royal Oak. Some of the people in the street used it when in funds but my father and mother were not among them. The pub was a two storeyed building, with a stable at the side although I never saw horses there. One difference between the pub and the rest of the street was that the brickwork had been painted cream which made it stand out from the long façade of varying shades of red or grey.

Adjoining the pub was another gaunt terrace of six houses with three storeys and very small windows. Among the families in this row were the Liversidges, the Coombes, the Collins and the Beauchamps. Mr. Beauchamp was a pub regular who got very noisy when in his cups. His poor, hard suffering wife used to work every day at the laundry to pay for his excesses. A small cottage was next to the terrace houses and like them had no garden but just a tiny yard and then came a doorway leading to the flat over the archway of Dean's Yard. This property had been well built, the archway was some fifteen feet in height and about ten feet in width. To protect the double doors when they were open to allow the passage of vehicles, two large stones about fifteen inches square and three feet in height had been placed next to the brickwork by the pavement. We often used to squat on them until chased away by Mr. Dean who was a horse dealer.

His yard, where the horses were stabled, went behind the houses and the pub through to Garden Cottages. He was a large red-faced gentleman who always carried a whip which he would use on anyone trespassing on his property. In contrast his wife was a neat quiet lady who was kind to small boys. Their home was on the other side of the archway, then came a terrace of five two-storey houses with attics, rather more modern than most in the street; in the first of these, Mr. & Mrs. Joe Chambers lived with their daughter. Joe was a bookbinder, a very highly skilled craftsman, so well thought of by his employers, Browns of the Canal, that when the business was sold to W.H. Smith's in 1924 they made a condition that Joe should continue in his department until retirement. Smith's closed the bookbinding section on his death in 1945.

Also living in this terrace were the Kellow, Bundy and Cool families. Mr. Bundy, a jobbing gardener, was about five feet in height but built like a tank whilst Mr. Cool, a clerk at Style and Gerrish, the main drapers in Salisbury, was a very quiet man who rose to be head of the firm's Accounts Department.

At the end of this terrace was a brick wall some ten feet in height behind which were the gardens of the Milford Hill houses, the first of these was on the corner of the streets.

I've mentioned that between the house where we lived, Number Forty Eight Culver Street and Number Forty Six were two large double doors, giving access to "The Cellar" which not only ran under both houses but also under Numbers Fifty and Fifty Two. There is no doubt in my mind that it was old — very, very old and I would think pre-dated the houses by several hundred years. Perhaps originally it had been the cellar of a Merchant's House, for it had walls varying between three and four feet in thickness, whereas the walls of the house where I spent my boyhood were only one brick or nine inches thick. The cellar had beautifully rounded arches leading to different sections which did not correspond to the dividing walls of the houses above. The apex of the arches was only some five feet six inches above floor level, indicating that either the floor had risen during repairs or men had become taller over the centuries.

In the twenties, the cellar was leased to The Haunch of Venison Inn in Minster Street, run by a man having a most unusual name Firmin S. Bradbeer. His cellarman who had to make the journey to Culver Street at least twice a day was an ex-City Police Sergeant named Golding. Sergeant Golding had unfortunately, after many years police service, blotted his copybook in about 1910, for when called to the scene of a local murder, he allowed the victim's mother, a widow, to clean up the room before detectives arrived. This serious "faux pas" brought the judge's wrath on Sergeant Golding and the mother who had been charged with her son's murder was acquitted — the case was never solved.

From the time that I was about ten, I used to look forward to Mr. Golding's visits, for sometimes on never-to-be-forgotten occasions he would let me go down into the cellar with him. Many a wet day was passed in this way for he let me help him, or did I hinder? I would stand at the street door and wait until his tall, burly figure appeared, still plodding along with that measured tread acquired from years on the beat. Unless it was pouring with rain he wore no hat or coat, his shirt sleeves rolled up to the elbow and wearing a green baize apron. His handcart must have been specially constructed for the job, having a concave, oval shaped base to take a barrel, whilst at either end were flat floors for crates. Mr. Golding usually had a smile and when he saw me would say, "Goin' to help me today, then Arthur?" I never needed a second bidding. My friends who lived nearby were all envious for I was the only one who had ever been down into the depths of the mysterious cellar.

Just inside the double doors were the stairs having wide steps and divided into two by a centre well in which was a rack. On each side of the stairs were flat sections of metal to take the runners of a lift operated by a pinion wheel on the rack. The lift used to go up and down in a very slow stately fashion just like a cliff railway. The motive power was by hand — there was a crank on either side at the bottom, though Mr. Golding was a powerful man, he was hard put to it to operate the lift on his own and used to puff whilst doing it. The lift was absolutely essential for some of the barrels were extremely large being brought from the Goods Station on horse-drawn drays and then manoeuvred to the road on specially constructed ramps which clipped to bars at the back of the carts. It was a very tricky operation to get the barrels safely down on to the road, up onto and across the pavement to the lift.

On one occasion the job went wrong, the huge barrel slipped from the ramp, split and best beer gushed from about half-way down the side on to the road and sped down the gutter. The news that some 1500 pints of bitter were going to waste soon brought a crowd of every kind and sort with every kind and sort of receptacle in which to catch some of the precious liquid. It was laughable to see grown men and women almost fighting to get a share of the booty. One lady even came armed with a floral chamber pot — she had obviously heard of the 14/20 Hussars Mess Dinners where a similar receptacle, but of silver is used for drinking. The only calm person around was Mr. Golding who stood arms akimbo, looking every inch the retired policeman and saying,

"It's alright — the insurance company will pay."

The cellar was packed with wine in bottles, wine in casks and barrels of beer, stout and cider. I used to help wash bottles, both pint and half pint size, standing on a crate by the machine which had a deep tank. On either side was a revolving brush, and the bottles had to be thrust onto these and held firmly in place for about five seconds. Then they went into another tank of clean water and from there into an oven to dry. The oven had an open front to avoid overheating. Beer was bottled each day, then labelled and put into crates. Mr. Golding seemed to take much more care when bottling wine. It was drawn from a cask, a cork inserted in the top of the bottle which was placed in the corking machine, one pull on the lever and home went the cork. Next they went to another small machine where a foil cap was forced firmly against the neck of the bottle. Now the bottle was labelled, rolled into a tray of dust, there was plenty of this in the cellar, for as Mr. Golding said "Nobody likes to think wine is freshly drawn."

Those hours spent with Mr. Golding are a very pleasant memory — he was always kind and must have been a nice type of man to allow a small boy to help, or should I say hinder him.

5 *Fire!*

When I was a small boy, quite serious fires seemed to occur in Salisbury with great frequency. This may have been caused by the heating and lighting used at that time, or perhaps modern communications plus far better fire fighting methods available today ensure that incidents are tackled much more quickly. Prior to the Second World War, the Salisbury Volunteer Fire Brigade, with the reputation of being a very efficient unit, had only a very small permanent staff which I believe varied between two and four firemen.

Early in 1921, a slight chill and a few spots on my chest meant that I was away from school for a couple of days. When I went back on the Wednesday, Miss Hale, the Headmistress of the Infants' School asked why I had been absent. When I mentioned spots on my chest, she sent me home again — no doubt having visions of an epidemic of chicken pox or measles. On my return home Mum said,

"Fancy telling Miss Hale that — well come on then, we'll go up and see where the big fire was."

She was not the only one with the same idea, because on arriving at Clarendon Road there was quite a sizeable crowd, just gazing at the still smouldering ruin of a terrace of five houses. The fire which had started early that morning must have been very fierce as only the walls were left standing and from the ruins there was that horrible fire-damp smell which pervades the site for weeks after such an occurrence. Watching at the scene was one of the unfortunate residents, Mr. Worby, manager of the Co-operative Society's Outfitting Department where I was often taken to buy clothes. He must have been very shortsighted for I remember the way in which he always peered through his very thick spectacles. Rumours were flying around as to how the fire started. The blame seemed to be directed towards one of the residents — a lady, separated from her husband, who was known to return home in the early hours. As I've grown older, I never cease to be amazed at the theories of the amateur detectives who always turn up at any tragic occurrence and immediately are able to give all the answers.

The fire brigade were very critical of the water pressure available to them in fighting this hilltop fire. They had resorted to laying a hose all the way to the River Bourne half-a-mile away. The following week tests were carried out and I went with Dad to watch the Brigade endeavouring to pump water to the roof of Blooms the Drapers on The Canal — possibly the City's tallest building. This they failed to do — I don't know how the problem was resolved — possibly by the purchase of a new engine.

At about the same time that I went up into the Boys' School, my friend Hubert Gould moved away to Bournemouth and my other friend Alf Norris moved from The Friary to Greencroft Street and, as this was only two hundred yards from our house, we saw quite a lot of each other. He now lived on the other side of the road from the Greencroft so it was very convenient for games of football or cricket. On a Saturday morning in June of 1922 I called for him but before we could play he had to go to Redmans, the butchers in Winchester Street, for his mother. We set off via Salt Lane and St. Edmund's Church Street and, like all small boys, saw much of interest on the way. The Salisbury Steam Laundry had just taken a delivery of fuel and the covers to the boiler room were open. By kneeling on the pavement, we could see the two furnaces being stoked but this innocent pastime was cut short by the boilerman who swore at us!

Next day — Sunday, was very hot and everyone went to bed with the windows wide open. At about 2 o'clock in the morning of Monday we were awakened by terrific shouting in the street and, when we looked out, the sky was just a red glow. The Steam Laundry was on fire. People were dashing along the roads in their night attire having just thrown on coats, my father went off first, next my mother and my Aunt Gertrude who lived with us.

Then I remember the shout of "Billy Roles' place is going up now" — this was Roles the Builders whose yard was opposite the laundry. The excitement was too much for my two sisters who had been left to look after me. Off they went to the corner of the street to see if they could see anything. I was left in bed trying not to show how scared I was — shivering and wondering how long it would be before our own

The Salisbury Steam Laundry in St Edmund's Church Street, after the disastrous fire of 12th June, 1922.

house caught fire, as from my window I could see the flames from the burning laundry, less than three hundred yards away. I also wondered — I was only seven — if the fire had anything to do with Alf Norris and I looking into the boiler room the day before!

By daylight the fire was almost under control. Fortunately little damage was done to Roles' Builders Yard, but the Steam Laundry was almost completely destroyed.

After school the following afternoon, Alf Norris and I made a beeline to see the damage. People were gazing at the still smoking ruins and chalked on a blackboard on the pavement was, "Employees meeting at Victoria Hall, Rollestone Street tonight at 6 o'clock." I went home and reported this to Mum who explained to me that the fire meant that a lot of people would now be out of work until the Laundry was rebuilt. Actually this was done in double-quick time but I can never forget the excitement and the terror of that night.

Each year, Bonfire Night was the highlight of early winter and I was fortunate enough to live within a quarter of a mile of The Greencroft, which became the mecca on November 5th for people from all parts of the City.

For more than a week before the great day we were collecting anything that would burn and literally dozens of individual fires began taking shape in what was known amongst boys as 'The Crot'. Some of the older ones would get together so that they had ginormous piles of rubbish. We would pray for fine weather as a prolonged wet spell meant ruin for our efforts. Although some skulduggery did go on, by and large no-one pinched material from someone else's fire — it was an unwritten law which was drummed into us at school "to keep your hands from picking and stealing" and this was obeyed by most youngsters.

As the day grew ever nearer the excitement mounted and if November 5th fell at a weekend, we had an added bonus because the whole of Saturday could be spent in topping up. Another unwritten law was that no fire was lit before dark, so the period of dusk on the great day seemed never ending.

During my first year at the Boys' School in 1922, Bonfire Night was held on a Saturday; November 5th falling on a Sunday that year. My special school friend Alf Norris lived in Greencroft Street and only the road separated his house from The Crot. We spent days building our fire right opposite and only about fifteen yards from his front door — never was anything so well watched. We thought we had an enormous pile but unfortunately our fire was not very long lasting and by 6 o'clock we were wandering about looking at the other, more professionally built conflagrations. Then I had a bright idea — why not go home to see if any more rubbish was available. Off the pair of us dashed and so were our hopes as of course nothing had been left uncollected. We decided to return to the Crot and ran into the Bruton brothers, Ron and Reg, who said they would come along with us. We had reached the corner of Guilder Lane and Winchester Street when a man hailed us with,

"Hey, you boys, you going up The Greencroft?"

I found out afterwards that the man was Mr. Mould, known as Tammy, who with his two spinster sisters ran "Moulds Dining Rooms" in Winchester Street. When we replied yes — he said,

"Come on, I've got something for you."

We went with our newly found friend who took us through the side door to a shed at the back of his premises and showed us what could only be described as treasure - five large horse collars of black leather. Each one seemed to weigh a ton at least to four small eight-year-olds. Someone had a bright idea — "let's put 'em round our necks." This we did and carried the remaining one between us - sort of a boy at each corner, that is if a horseshoe shape has corners. We started off and although with only about 200 yards to go, had constant stops and changing of places. However eventually we got there — our own fire was out and off we went towards one of the largest of the evening. There we were welcomed as if the old collars were of great value. They were thrown to the top of the furnace and burned away merrily.

I got home that night full of excitement, a state which was quickly changed when my mother discovered that I was well and truly inundated with horse fleas. A bath was quickly prepared and, after being thoroughly scrubbed, had to suffer the indignity of having my hair cleaned with a nit comb — a most painful operation. Never mind it was a wonderful evening. Looking back, it seems a marvel that the houses surrounding the Greencroft were never set on fire — the residents must have suffered very anxious hours, but for the rest of us the sight of so many fires all blazing away was one never forgotten.

On a very fine and hot Saturday in September 1925, a Cubs' Football Match was in progress at Shady Bower, the playing field belonging to St. Martin's Church. Suddenly, at about 3 o'clock, a pall of thick black smoke could be seen rising from the town and shortly afterwards came flames and then loud crackling was heard. We all rushed to the wire fence overlooking Milford Station and I remember Miss Joyce Brown, our cubmistress saying,

"I wonder if it's a fire that ought to be!"

One of our cubs was Ernie Truckle who lived in Gigant Street, next to Young's Timber Yard. Whilst we were still looking at the blaze, Marjorie Truckle (Ernie's sister), who would have been about thirteen years of age, came rushing across the field with a message from their mother —

"Could Ernie go home at once as Youngs was on fire."

The football match was abandoned and we all dashed to Gigant Street to see the blaze. When we got there the street was crowded with people who must have come from all parts of the City. Not for the first time Salisbury found it was easy to attract a large audience for a free show. One small memory stands out: in the street was a treadle sewing machine, removed from one of the houses and on the top of this item rescued from possible loss by fire — two quite green apples.

Young's Yard ran behind five houses fronting Gigant Street and backed onto Farr's Coachbuilding Works in Brown Street. Imagine my horror when I found out that the fire had now spread to this building, where my father worked. I made my way through the crowds to Farr's in Brown Street, managed to get right up to the entrance and poke my head around the door to see what was going on. I had just seen Dad and another man carrying a tool box to safety when a loud shout from a policeman sent me scurrying back from my vantage point.

By half-past four the fire was almost over. Two sizeable works had gone in under two hours, although it was forty-eight hours before new outbreaks ceased. It was almost a year before Farr's was rebuilt and my father worked at his forge in the open air right through the winter. The coach work was carried on in the trimming shop which was in Friary Lane but, from then on, Farr"s business was on a downward path, finally closing in 1929.

It was during this incident that I became aware of Husseys Hatches, as the Fire Brigade used the water from one of these, nearly opposite the Brown Street Baptist Church. These hatches were openings to an underground stream running from Castle Street via Scots Lane and Bedwin Street then, after a right hand diversion via Rollestone Street, Brown Street and the Friary to join the River Avon again near Riverside Walk. Alderman Hussey was Mayor of the City in 1758 and he would have been pleased that his idea of bringing a clean water supply to St. Edmund's and St. Martin's Parishes was still quite useful almost 170 years later. The hatches were also brought into use in the 1939-1945 war.

6 *The Day of Rest*

Back in the 'twenties, Sunday at our home was a day apart and, as far as was possible, the Sabbath had to be kept as ordered in the Fourth Commandment. If it happened to be the first Sunday in the month my mother, my Aunt Gertrude and my two sisters (after their respective confirmations) went to early service — 7 o'clock Holy Communion at the Parish Church of St. Martin's.

Before leaving for church, it was a ritual to drink a cup of tea which was supposed to ward off a fainting attack during the service. As Holy Communion was by tradition the first food and drink of the day, the tea left a feeling of guilt for I was told never to tell anyone although I expect it was a common practice amongst lady communicants.

Immediately after the service my aunt would dash to work at Nelson House, one of the Godolphin School Boarding Houses, whilst my mother and sisters came home to breakfast, already prepared by Dad, and in winter time he would also have the kitchen fire blazing away.

After breakfast, the first washing-up of the day and then Mum and the girls would start to prepare dinner, for everyone except the elite had "dinner" in the middle of the day. During the summer Dad would go to the allotment or at other times of the year start one or other of the jobs which he always seemed to have to do. It appeared to me that the only thing he had never mastered was paper hanging. As for me it was preparation for Morning Service at 10.30 am. The Sunday School sat in the North Aisle and everyone had to take the same seat week by week. At the end of each row was the monitor who marked the attendance which, if regular, entitled you to a Prize at the end of the year, a book chosen from a list by the recipient and presented at the Annual Service on Low Sunday. I still have a number of these in my possession.

A few minutes before the start of the service, the girls from three of the Godolphin Boarding Houses would arrive under the eagle eyes of several mistresses, who always seemed to wear stern expressions. The girls *en masse* looked extremely smart especially in the summer, when they wore cream straw boaters, having a bright red band, white blouses, navy blue skirts and white gloves. They marched in pairs through the west door, made a right turn, followed by a left turn and very quickly almost filled the complete length of the South Aisle. No talking was allowed, neither could they communicate with anyone except their school companions outside the church. The girls from Beckingsale House sat in the pews right at the back, their clothing resembling prison uniform. In the meantime the nave would be three-quarters filled with the rest of the congregation. How different to the empty churches of today.

When we left at 11.20 am the forecourt would be crowded with another congregation waiting to enter for the 11.30 am Celebration of the Sung Eucharist.

From the time that I was eight years of age, on coming out from Morning Service, I could not hang about with my friends, but had to dash to the Sunday Newspaper seller who operated a pitch outside Wilkes, Son and Cassey's Ironmongers Shop on the corner of Milford Street and Queen Street. Newspaper shops did not open on Sundays in the 'twenties. After all, Salisbury is a Cathedral City and at that time Sunday was well observed. I had to buy *The People* and *The News of the World* which was then even more of a scandal sheet than it is today. I started my long walk, interspersed with running sessions to deliver the papers to Mr. Brooks, the Head Gardener at Godolphin School, who lived right at the bottom of Laverstock Road, a distance of almost a mile. Mr. Brooks, a friend of Dad's, suffered from corns and so was unable to make the journey to buy his own papers without considerable discomfort. When I arrived, he would be waiting and was always so pleased. I think the papers made his day, perhaps he relished scandal. Anyway I was given sixpence, fourpence for the papers and tuppence for myself.

When I got back home I had to don my apron to protect my Sunday best clothes. This was a scaled-down version of the carpenter's apron worn by my father on the Sabbath.

Dinner was at 1 o'clock — always a roasted joint with beautifully baked potatoes and very special gravy. Special because of the secret ingredient which was a dessert spoonful of sugar, held in the top of the fire until it flamed, when it would be stirred rapidly in the gravy, a job that I liked doing. The same spoon had been used for this for many years and was burnt black. There was a fruit pie of some sort with delicious crust pastry — each helping covered with freshly made piping hot custard.

Dad always did the washing up on Sundays and we children all had our jobs. Whilst my sisters wiped up, from an early age I was given the task of transporting the clean china and utensils from the lid of the copper (there was no draining board) to the kitchen table for one of the adults to put away.

After dinner there was little spare time before I made my way to Sunday School, held in St. Martin's Boys' School. This started at 2.30 pm, lasted for an hour and was under the direction of Mr. Ernest Russ, our Headmaster. However, during the holidays at Easter, Whitsun, Summer and Christmas we went to church for a Service taken by one of the clergy and in Mr. Russ's absence, Miss Frances Awdry would be in charge.

There was little time for dalliance when we came out from Sunday School as I was expected to be home for tea at half-past four. In any case, most games were taboo whilst wearing your Sunday clothes. The thing which put Sunday tea apart from that of the rest of the week was the lovely hot Wiltshire dough cake. This would have been delivered on Saturday evening by Mr. Bishop of Woodfords, the Downton bakers, who also made a delivery on Tuesdays. The reason that my mother continued to patronise Woodfords, whilst surrounded by Salisbury bakers, went back to 1857, when the founder of the firm canvassed door to door in Salisbury and happened to call on my great-grandmother in Rollestone Street. He stated that it was his intention to start a Salisbury delivery but great-grandmother said that whilst she wouldn't change, her daughter who was about to marry might be interested. Either Mr. Woodford had a twinkle in his eye or was just a good salesman, but the upshot was that he supplied my grandmother over many years, in his turn his son carried on and continued serving my mother, right up to 1949 when the Salisbury round had only two customers left.

After tea — more washing up with Dad at the helm and little time was left before the whole family were off to Evensong at St. Martin's where my father was a sidesman for a number of years. It was common practice for families to attend evening service and we sat in the same pew each week, about half way back in the north aisle. Mum sat at the end nearest the wall, then my two sisters, whilst I sat next to Dad, who took the outside seat ready for a quick get-away when it was time to take the collection. The seat in front of us was occupied by a blind man, Mr. Shergold, who lived in Love Lane. It was uncanny the way that he always knew when he reached the pew. He was fetched from his home by Mr. Ted Warren, one of Dad's old friends.

At St. Martin's the Festivals were always celebrated at Evensong by a procession around the Church during the final hymn, when the four banners were carried. The two largest of these were especially fine — one representing the Patron Saint as a Roman Soldier on horseback, cutting his cloak in half and giving a half to a beggar.

After church, if it was winter, we went straight home where we were often joined by some of Mum's old friends, mostly unmarried. There did seem to be a lot of spinsters in the twenties. Sometimes my sisters would play the piano but the music had to be of the kind suitable for Sunday. I remember my father's favourite — a rather nostalgic piece called, "The Hymns my mother used to sing".

On fine evenings in summer, we always took a walk after church, usually by the same route, which was up St. Martin's Lane and Fowlers Hill to Milford Hollow. Down over the railway footbridge, past Milford Manor to Milford Bridge. Once we reached the far side of the bridge we went via a very old iron kissing gate into the field which early in summer was always a mass of buttercups. Through the field was a footpath that led via another similar gate to the next field dominated by a line of magnificent elms which were uprooted during the great storm of 1930. At the end of the path another kissing gate brought you to the rough farm lane running past Milford House, owned by the Ware family, the Salisbury leather magnates. Turning right along the lane brought you to Southampton Road by Dairyhouse Bridge, another right turn and along the main road to another footpath opposite Waterloo Gardens — this led into the churchyard and so to home. At that time the whole walk from Milford Hollow was in unspoilt country, even the Southampton Road section possessed no buildings whereas today it is completely built up.

Another lovely walk that the family occasionally took was to West Harnham or as it was known locally "Watery Harnham", a fitting nickname for there was always plenty in the rivers, streams and water meadows.

Upon leaving church we set off via Paynes Hill, Barnard's Street, Trinity Street, Ivy Street and New Street to Crane Street. These six streets formed almost a straight line, but from the medieval stone bridge, still having the old ford on the Fisherton side, the road curved to the Iron Bridge which crossed one of the branches of the River Avon as it flowed out from Water Lane. Until the nineteen-fifties this stream continued alongside Harcourt Bridge Road to join the River Nadder at Long Bridge, but has now been diverted, looking more like a canal as it dissects Elizabeth Gardens. Long Bridge in those days was quite a rickety wooden structure, which shook as you walked across. The Nadder seemed to carry much more water that used to go under the bridge at a fair old pace.

We continued via the footpath beside a stream where the water, although almost still, was beautifully clear, revealing a bed of soft fine mud. Eventually we came to the Old Mill area where there were no railings at the waterside, making the mill pond quite a frightening place for small children. If the hatches behind the mill were open, the main stream of the Nadder would rush through and drop some six or seven feet rather like a waterfall. On the far side of the pond was the old ford and Mum used to tell us that this was the route to the city taken by carts before the building of the old Harnham Bridge in the fourteenth century, although I expect it was used right up to the advent of the motor car.

The footpath went over the hatches to the Mill, at that time a bone-mill which produced a terrible smell that pervaded a wide area, rather spoiling the lovely spot. The pong was such that we used to pinch our noses as we ran past. Another set of hatches by the back wall of the building, when opened sent more water spuming under the mill to reappear in the wide pond to the front.

We would make our way past The Three Crowns Inn where people sat on forms by wooden tables to enjoy a summer's evening drink. From then on, the walk was far less interesting: we passed the Bishops Wordsworth School Sports Field then came a long dull stretch to The Rose and Crown, that always looked decrepit until renovation in the 'thirties. Then we went over the two Harnham Bridges, one with its niches to enable pedestrians to shelter from passing vehicles and so to

Exeter Street and home.

Taking a Sunday evening stroll was a regular family pastime, an enjoyable occasion that is unfortunately seldom seen today.

There was for a period of some two months or so in the summer of 1922 a diversion which my mother and aunt enjoyed after the walk. This was due to the advent of "Bee" wine. Why it got this name I've no idea, as the so called "bees", looking rather like the cereal Sugar Puffs, were reputed to be an Australian fungus with yeast-like properties. To get started on the making of the wine you needed three or four bees which were freely available from friends or neighbours, you filled a jam jar with water to about half an inch from the top, added two desert spoonfuls of sugar, placed the "bees" on the water, covered with muslin and waited for a fortnight. During that period the bees would be working busily up and down in the fermenting liquid and at the end of the two weeks it was ready for straining and bottling. Now you not only had the wine but also found that the bees had multiplied, so that you could start off three or four jars. After another fortnight you had enough for twelve or sixteen.

It was manna from heaven. Most houses had rows of jars with fermenting liquid — the only losers were the pubs who just could not compete with this almost free wine, which I remember — I had a sip or two when no-one was looking, was of sweet taste but with a real kick. My mother and aunt used to have two small glasses apiece, the result being that poor dad was left to get supper. My father would not touch the stuff, he said it might be poisonous. He could have been right at that, when one considers the trips that hippies take after eating some types of mushroom. The bonanza went on until the church thought enough was enough and so on a Sunday evening in August, a concerted effort was made and strong sermons were preached from every pulpit against bee wine and its evil effects. As a result my mother went home and poured away all her stock. Funnily enough, I think the craze has never resurfaced in the seventy years since that time.

7 *Some City Streets*

When I was a boy Milford Street always seemed very busy, maybe because it was the nearest main thoroughfare to my Culver Street home. The Milford Hill section between Culver Street and Rampart Road was mainly private housing with the exception of White's Baker's Shop on the Guilder Lane corner and St. Martin's Men's Club on the south corner with Rampart Road.

Near the club entrance were two old houses and in one of these lived the local bird catcher. In the 'twenties the list of protected birds was small and this gentleman, Mr. Thomas, did quite a trade in song-birds which he used to catch on the downs around the city. His front window was packed with small cages containing linnets, greenfinches, bullfinches and song thrushes amongst others. Eventually the law caught up with him and he was heavily fined for caging protected species.

Tucked in by the side of the club was a tiny house, reached via a narrow path about three feet wide. I remember that the occupant — a very old, very small man — spent all his time leaning over the gate, watching the world go by.

Right opposite the club was a court containing about ten houses, built against the old city rampart. The front doors were some eight feet above the court surface so each pair of dwellings had a flight of steep brick steps leading to them. I recall the houses as Bill Scutt, the senior cub in my pack, lived in one of them.

The next section between Culver Street and Gigant Street and Guilder Lane and Pennyfarthing Street could have seen little change over a long period. On the south side at the Culver Street corner was Jenkins, the grocers and just below this Penns, Wholesale Confectioners, who also ran a retail shop in Catherine Street. Quite near were some very old and very decrepit buildings occupied by Talbots, Wholesale Chemists and Druggists. Although there was never a great deal of action, at one time the firm must have done a fair trade as old Mr. Talbot was reputed to be a very wealthy man. He was the main shareholder in a business on the opposite side of the street, Ivamy's, Job Masters, and each morning would drive to work from his Manor Road home in one of their horse drawn cabs. He would sit bolt upright, wearing a top hat which was unusual headgear for the Salisbury of the 'twenties. The old gentleman was a continual critic of the City Council and started in the late 'twenties, in conjunction with Mr. Allan B. Lemon, the well-known Salisbury Solicitor, a Salisbury Ratepayers' Association. The Ratepayers' Magazine could be described as a local "Private Eye". Another of Mr. Talbot's activities was the loaning of money at a fair old rate of interest but he did not believe in spending a penny to smarten his premises from which the paint was peeling so badly that bare wood was revealed.

Next to Talbot's was The George Herbert Elementary School which from 1919, became a girls-only institution, the boys being taught at St. Martin's. The school seemed cold and it was certainly dark for the main windows faced north and tall buildings surrounded it on the other three sides. Just below George Herbert's lived Mr. Player, a wood turner who was a master craftsman noted for superb work — samples in his window included twist chair and table legs, candlesticks and even wooden eggs. He was quite a small man, about five feet in height, poor and shabby-looking. His walk was very brisk and he always carried a preoccupied expression as if his mind was centred on the way the next work of art might be tackled. At the Gigant Street corner was Mrs. Goodfellow's Newsagent's shop. She was a war widow with one daughter Olive who attended The High School in London Road. The shop was well below pavement level for there were two steps down inside the door. I remember that whenever I had tuppence to spend I used to go there to buy one of the outdated paperbacks from the "Popular Sports Library" on sale at half-price. Each book ran to 64 pages and from these gems I learnt a great deal about Soccer, Cricket, Rugby Union, Rugby League and other sports. It was good boys' stuff — the hero always scoring the winning goal, hit or try.

On the opposite Gigant Street corner were the offices of Gibbs Mew, whilst next came the large, well-proportioned Milford Street United Methodist Church, fronted by cast iron railings above a low wall. The church attracted quite large congregations and the Sunday

Although this photograph of Milford Street was taken at the turn of the century, the buildings showed little alteration in the 'thirties.

School not only offered pupils a full day trip to the sea during the summer but also splendid Christmas treats, thus somewhat upstaging the Anglicans who had a half day trip to the New Forest with an ordinary Christmas Tea. I don't suppose these incentives made a deal of difference to the attendance as families were either "church" or "chapel" and never the twain shall meet. My mother, who came from a staunchly "church" family, used to express her antipathy when she often declared, "He's nothing but a chapel dodger," and it's difficult to describe the scorn that she would put into the phrase.

Mr. Uphill's butcher shop, adjoined the Methodist Church, it was small, very clean and well scrubbed. The proprietor's brother was the only employee and, although a married man with a family, he seemed to spend more than half his time delivering orders on the almost universal tradesman's bike, with its large wicker basket and the triangular sign carrying the owner's name fixed to the frame. The boss, Mr. Uphill, always had his sleeves rolled up way past the elbows —

whether for comfort or to exhibit the many tattoos which covered his arms is anyone's guess. Then came the William IV public house, an old two-storied building noted for its sideline of hiring handcarts for tuppence an hour. These had been acquired by the licensee when Frank Cooper, the Coachbuilder of Brown Street, retired. My father had been apprenticed to Mr. Cooper and he told me that the trucks had been made when trade was slack. As the trucks were some twenty-odd years old when I was small and were still going strong forty years later, they must have paid for themselves over and over again.

The confectionery shop next door was owned by a bachelor named White. His two unmarried sisters were in the same line of business in Winchester Street, but whilst their tiny shop was always an advertisement for cleanliness, his was quite the opposite. The window had, during the summer months, more than its fair share of flies, whilst the proprietor was never to be seen in the shop without a flat black cap on his head and cigarette end dangling from the corner of his mouth. His moustache was nicotine — stained on either end and, in later years, a dewdrop at the end of his nose completed the dismal picture. Needless to say Mr. White's establishment was not well patronised.

When I was a very small boy, the shop next to Mr. White was a fishmongers but in the early twenties it was acquired by Mr. & Mrs. Prewett who opened a fish and chip establishment. There you could buy a pennyworth of chips and a piece of cod for tuppence — served on a plate if you wished. The Cecil Cafe next door was run by Mr. Gray and then came The Goat public house, which after closure in 1927 became a hotch-potch of offices and workshops, used by small traders. Adjoining was a sizeable grocers — Tom Oke's, whilst at the Brown Street Corner came Snelgars, the Corn and Seed Merchants. One of my Saturday jobs as a youngster was to fetch seven pounds of Mixed Corn from this shop. By the time I got back home that seven pounds felt like seventy and I shall never forget, when I was about eight years old, with only a few yards to go, I dropped the precious parcel. The brown paper bag tied with white string hit the pavement, split and corn went all over the place. In tears, I fetched my father who went to work with a shovel and retrieved most of the contents.

On the opposite corner of Brown Street were Soffes' Tea Rooms, next came Chaplin's offices. They were carriers to the Southern Railway although Suttons handled the smaller parcels. Chaplin's also issued railway tickets. Adjoining was the travellers' room belonging to The Red Lion Hotel. This was used by representatives to display goods to prospective local buyers, a practice continued until the late 'fifties. The Red Lion Milford Street façade has changed little over the years but the adjoining shop at the Catherine Street corner has had a number of owners in different retail trades. In the twenties, Mr. Cripps, described by A.G. Street as the "prince of grocers", was still carrying on the old established business. A small, happy man with a white beard, he always wore the traditional grocers' apron. The shop had that lovely smell which one associates with his type of establishment and the floor was always sprinkled with fresh sawdust. I also remember the stone lettering on the shop's Milford Street wall announcing Cripps Tea and Grocery Warehouse. Each letter was some twenty-four inches high and five inches in thickness and styled in a very ugly heavy block which although perhaps in vogue from 1860 to 1880 was distinctly

Mr Cripps standing with one of his assistants at the door of his grocery shop, on the corner of Milford Street and Catherine Street. (Note the sawdust on the floor and the massive stone lettering on the wall to the left.)

outmoded by 1920. It was not an inexpensive place to shop but each Christmas my mother went there to buy her annual oval shaped bottle of Tarragona wine. This was a rich port type and the bottle holding about a quart cost 3s9d.

On the corner of Milford Street with Queen Street was a large ironmongers, Wilkes, Son and Cassey, one of five similar shops trading in the city centre. As was customary a number of items such as galvanised baths, water cans and garden implements were hung on hooks outside, below the fascia. Even baskets of oddments were placed on the pavement, a practice which would be frowned on today, but the footpaths were kept spotlessly clean by each trader. This was not only a matter of pride but was also done to conform to the old City by-law which called for the cleansing of pavements by 3 p.m. each day. This by-law has never been repealed and it is a great pity that it is not still rigidly enforced. The firm of Wilkes, Son and Cassey ceased trading in 1926, the business and premises were purchased by The Salisbury Co-operative Society Limited who then only stocked larger items of ironmongery and added a furniture department on the first floor.

The Cathedral Hotel, next door, was also at one time in the hands of the Wilkes family and it first came to my notice when an extra floor was added in 1922/23. The wiseacres — and there were many, my own father among them — forecast a collapse of the building: "The foundations ain't never going to stand it." An event that never happened, although there was a scare during the extremely fierce fire at the Co-operative Society's shop in 1937 when cracks were noticed in the hotel's adjoining wall.

A newsagent's shop came next. This was acquired in the early 'twenties by the Noyce family and they continued trading there for the next sixty years. A small drapers, "Palmers", was next door but after a few years this became a Baby Wear shop. Adjoining was Mr. Baker's Tailoring and Outfitting Establishment. I remember the senior assistant, Mr. Parsons who worked there for almost his whole life. His son, Wilfred, a pupil-teacher at St. Martin's, taught me during my first year in the Boys' School. Bakers have of course extended to the Brown Street corner, but in the twenties had Mr. Denham, the baker as neighbour, a beautifully clean shop which traded until the late 1940s when it was taken over by W. Shipsey and Sons.

Right on the Brown Street corner was The Round of Beef public house which was closed by Eldridge Pope & Co., the Dorchester Brewers in 1926 when it remained empty for several years. In 1931, following the death of Mr. Hugh Morrison, the Member of Parliament for Salisbury, it was purchased by the local Conservative Association. Following demolition, a memorial hall, named after the late member was erected on the site.

H. Till and Son, who occupied the opposite Brown Street Corner, were well known saddlers and also sold extremely high-class leather goods. The workshop where saddles were made by hand had to be enlarged in the 'thirties and the adjoining Hinwoods Garage was acquired where passers-by could watch the craftsmen at work. The small shop next to Tills was run by Mr. Charlie Wigley, a boot and shoe repairer who became, each Saturday afternoon during the football season, the popular inside left for St. Martin's, three times winners of The Wiltshire Junior Cup in the early 'twenties.

The only pawnbroker in Salisbury operated at No. 21 but closed in 1918. The shop was owned by Mr. Sewell who also ran a furniture store, further up the street at No. 29. During the 'twenties and 'thirties all sorts of items that were unredeemed pledges from the pawnbroking days appeared in the furniture shop windows. I well remember buying in 1926, for two shillings, a large pile of encyclopaedias, which had been issued in weekly parts in 1910. I had to save the purchase price, which took several weeks' pocket money and watched almost daily, hoping that no-one else would buy the books before I had enough cash. I was lucky, bought the books, took the treasure home and found they only covered A to M. Nevertheless I found them interesting and still thought they were a bargain.

Between Sewell's and The Brewery Tap was a greengrocer's shop that was acquired in about 1923 by the daughter and son-in-law of Mr. Tommy Sparks, who ran his Men's Hairdressing business at No. 31. The couple — Mr. and Mrs. Reeves — were both of very short stature, hardly touching five feet in height. The public house known as the Brewery Tap was quite a large and tall building having a big yard with stables at the left hand side. I recall as a boy watching in admiration as Mr. Harry Martin, the signwriter wrote The Brewery Tap all along the front of the building, some thirty feet above street level. The letters must have been at least two feet in height and to do this job from a ladder, with only a young apprentice to hold it steady was quite a feat.

Tommy Sparks with his extremely efficient-looking staff, outside his Milford Street shop, in the days when he catered for men only.

Today, several men would spend a considerable time erecting steel scaffolding before such a job would be attempted.

Sheppard Brothers ran a gents hairdressing shop at No. 27. It was indeed a performance to get your hair cut there as the two elderly unmarried brothers quite unwittingly put on a music hall act. Each repeated the other's remarks and on the couple of occasions that I went there when Sparks were crowded out, I found that it was extremely difficult not to laugh.

Next came Sewells Furniture Store and adjoining this was Mr. Tommy Sparks where I went for haircuts for over forty years. Prior to 1924 it was men only, then when ladies began to have short hair, a curtain was put across the shop and behind this was the third chair where Mr. Yeates, Tommy's recently acquired partner began operating on the female sex. Sparks and Yeates found that the new venture was something of a small goldmine, much more lucrative than cutting mens' and boys' hair for 6d and 3d respectively. The shop was quickly feminised to become ladies only whilst men and boys were relegated to a back room behind the Reeves greengrocery shop, further down the street. Here the business continued, almost unaltered for sixty years.

Tommy Sparks was a man having a remarkable thirst and woe betide anyone unfortunate enough to be having a haircut around opening time. It happened to me on one occasion when I was about ten. Tommy had started and trimmed one side of my head, then noticing that it was six o'clock said "Shan't be a minute" and was gone for ten. He came back, wiping his mouth with the back of his hand, said "That's better" and proceeded with the operation. I am sure that he lost many customers because of his habit of popping across the road to his favourite tippling place The William the Fourth.

Over the years, he told me on many occasions of his first day in business at Wilton when a young man. With all the confidence of youth, he had handbills printed that T. Sparks would be opening a Gentlemen's Hairdressing Saloon at Number so and so North Street. It was in fact the front room of a house. Tommy spent quite a time delivering the handbills to every house in the town and opened for business at eight o'clock on a Monday morning and closed twelve hours later. His total takings for the day amounted to one penny for a shave. He was so fed up that he put another penny to the one earned for a whole day's labour and went to the pub where he drowned his sorrows in a pint.

As a sideline, to fill in time when the shop was devoid of customers, Tommy repaired umbrellas on a bench tucked away in the corner. I don't think he was fitted for the job as it seemed to bring out the worst in him and his language used to become very picturesque. When he was semi-retired he sat on a chair in the corner of the saloon, gossiping away to his customers. If I went in, he would insist on cutting my hair himself and embarrass me by telling those waiting that he could remember cutting my first curls.

Adjoining Tommy Sparks was yet another pub, the street seemed to be full of them, this one was called The Catherine Wheel, an unusual name believed to have come from the eleventh century Knights of Saint Catherine of Mount Sinai. Next door was a tiny car showroom belonging to Goddard and Co, and I remember standing outside with Dad in 1922, admiring the first Austin Seven or "Baby Austin", as it was quickly named. It was an open tourer having a folding hood and never looked large enough to take four adults. The manager of Goddards, "Wiggy" Harris, had at one time been a teacher at the local "School of Art" where his father Mr. Joseph Harris was Headmaster. A small, thin, dapper man, he was totally bald and, as his nickname implies, wore a toupe. This was ginger brown in colour and so badly fitting that only a blind man would not realise that it was a hairpiece. "Wiggy" was however a first class businessman and, under his leadership, Goddard's grew to be one of the largest garages in the area.

On the Pennyfarthing Street corner was James Garage which had been a Job Masters with a showroom at the corner. The yard at the side had been roughly roofed over with corrugated iron; it was not entirely waterproof as buckets and other containers were dotted around the floor to catch the drips. "Peggy" James, the proprietor, a heavily built man and had a wooden leg — hence his nickname — but he was remarkably speedy to provide quick service when cars drew up for petrol from his one, hand-operated pump.

Now came yet another pub: The Crystal Fountain, which was quite a large three storeyed building, having a prominent bay window on the first floor. It always appeared to be the busiest of the seven in the street. At the side was a large gateway having two massive pillars from which hung double gates, each measuring some six feet in height by eight feet in width and constructed of heavy matchboard. These enclosed a long yard, at the end of which was Sainsbury's Warehouse. Sainsbury's were well known Wholesale Grocers with a head office at Trowbridge. They ran a fleet of slow, chain-driven lorries, a type that quickly went out of fashion in the 'twenties.

Ivamys the job masters yard was next to Sainsbury's entrance. They had about a dozen horse-drawn cabs and two hearses. When a small boy, I felt sorry for their horses, which were always black in colour, so that they could be put to use for funerals. Whatever the weather they spent most of the time waiting for fares, either at one or other of the Railway Stations or the cab ranks in Fisherton Street or Blue Boar Row. The day over, they went back to dark and dismal stables at the rear of the yard. I don't suppose life was a great deal better for their cabbies, who always looked poor and pinched.

Several old dwelling houses adjoined Ivamys but at the Guilder Lane corner was a small shop, taken over in 1922 by a Lancashire family called Farrer. Mr. Farrer, a white haired man in his fifties was stone deaf but fortunately could lip read, whilst his wife was a really excellent cook. In no time their home-made faggots at $1\frac{1}{2}$d each, Nelson cakes at 1d — they were like moist bread pudding with pastry at top and bottom, apple turnovers also at 1d each and similar items became more and more popular. The tiny room at the back of the shop was fitted with a trestle table and two forms and country people went there for a meal on market days. A few years later, the Farrers moved the flourishing business to premises over the Empire Meat Company in The Ox Row at the side of the Market Place and it continued there for the next thirty years. Faggots made today are not a patch on Mrs. Farrer's.

One thing that puzzled me as a boy was Mrs. Farrer's hair — it used to change overnight from snow white to jet black and a few days later it was white again. Must have been something connected with all the cooking! They had two children, the son, a motor engineer was forever trying to get old motorbikes to function, his greasy overalls being quite out of tune with the cleanliness of mother's shop. The daughter, Marjory was small, dark-haired and so bow-legged that to quote my father, "she would never stop a pig in a passage". She was busily engaged in courting Maurice Dawkins who lived in Culver Street and seemed to be always in the shop complaining of his drawbacks for all and sundry to hear. On one occasion when the poor chap was a few minutes late, it was, "He's only ever on time when he wants to take me to church."

I remember the gypsies or didycoys congregating outside their favourite pubs in Milford Street on Tuesdays and Saturdays which were both Market Days. The pubs most in favour seemed to be The Crystal Fountain, The Catherine Wheel, The Round of Beef and The Oddfellows Arms. Gypsy women would come into the City very early with large wicker baskets on each arm — laden on Tuesdays with home-made clothes pegs together with bits and pieces, but usually posies on Saturdays. They were always ready to tell fortunes and if asked, seemed to know a Romany cure for every ailment. The men were always conspicuous by their absence until shortly before the pubs were due to open. Then they were all friends together, but within an hour or two and a pint or two, or three or four, of rough cider or scrumpy, how their personalties changed. Then they were ready to fight the world, or at least the world within reach. One of the big troubles was the way that they obstructed the pavements as most of their drinking would be done in the street, sat with backs against the pub wall. At least this way they did not have far to fall. The police force generally left them alone, providing they kept the fighting amongst themselves.

Gigant Street was most interesting for it not only housed Gibbs Mew & Co's Brewery but also Tylee's Rag and Bone store or more correctly, as the large sign at the front of the building proclaimed, "C.E. TYLEE, Wool, Horsehair, Rag, Metal and Skin Merchant and Marine Store Dealer." I remember this sign for when a small boy, I was puzzled as to what Tylees could have to do with the sea. The store served a most useful purpose as Mr. Tylee would buy almost anything. Rabbit skins fetched 1d or 2d, depending on the season, jam jars were 1d for 6 of the one pound size, rags were worth more if sorted before selling, into wools and cottons whilst the price of scrap metal varied greatly.

Just inside the big double entrance doors were hundreds of tiles which never seemed to be sold. They were about nine inches by six inches, some two inches in thickness, with a bold diamond pattern, deeply cut into the hard black face. For many years they had formed part of The Market Place surface. Covering the brick floor were piles of scrap — rusty cracked drain pipes, guttering, old kitchen ranges, wooden tubs for oddments, such as nuts and bolts, square wicker baskets that held rabbit skins, cotton, wool, crates into which jam jars were stacked, the variety was endless. From the white washed wooden ceiling hung all sorts of items — lamps, cycle frames, farm and garden implements and dozens of other things. Presumably, Mr. Tylee considered these had not outlived their useful life and if he kept them long enough, a buyer might come along.

The store had a peculiar and not altogether wholesome odour, a cross between a creek when the tide is out and the smell produced by the local sewage works. In the yard at the back, a slow burning bonfire added to the pong which could not have been good for those living nearby.

Next to the Marine Store was Miss Tylee's shop — she was the sister of Mr. C.E. Tylee, but no-one would ever have guessed it, as her shop was one of the cleanest and tidiest that I have every seen. She sold a great variety of household goods, brushes of every type, string, rope, reels of cotton, thread, sylko, clothes pegs, dustpans, all sorts of things. She did quite a wholesale trade with pedlars who used to retail the goods door to door in the surrounding villages. Miss Tylee's courtesy was unfailing — she was a neatly dressed lady who wore a velvet neckband and her "pince-nez" or pinchers as we called them were attached to a thin gold necklet, ready to be placed at the end of her nose when she was searching for something required by her customers. Miss Tylee always gave a cheerful service and was most helpful; if she didn't stock an article the customer was always advised where it could be obtained.

Opposite her shop was the Church of St. Mary Magdalene, erected in 1880 as a chapel of ease for the Parish Church of St. Martin. It was a simply constructed building of corrugated iron with pine matchboard lining. The wooden framed windows were of Early English shape and at the east end was a small turret, surmounted by a tiny spire some ten feet in height. This too was of wooden construction. The church probably held some two hundred people but was not used a great deal in the 1920's. In fact, when the spire was blown down during a gale, early in 1925, it was not replaced. Just down the road on the same side was Mr. E.... W......'s Cycle Shop — although their elders warned small boys to keep away from this establishment, they never gave the reason.

Gigant Street had two pubs — The Gigant Street Brewery Tap and The Anchor Brewery Tap — and two general stores. One of these, Moody's, was on the corner with Trinity Street. The other, owned by Mrs. Whitlock, was a marvellous place. She was a war widow and worked round the clock in her efforts to bring up a young family by herself. The shop had a smell all of its own, quite indescribable, a mixture of greengrocery, vinegar, all the usual grocery smells plus the wafting odour from the Rag and Bone store almost next door. Mrs. Whitlock retained the pre-war length of dress, almost to the ground and

Mrs Whitlock's shop in Gigant Street — "a marvellous place."

covered by a voluminous apron made from discarded sugar sacks. She always had a cherry-red face, with cheery smile and was a great favourite with the youngsters of the area. Her home-made toffee apples were the real thing even though more often than not, when the coating was licked away, green fruit would be revealed and the sticks always look like cut down kindling wood, as they probably were. The soft drinks which she also made were good sellers during the summer months, costing only 2½d and even then, 1d was allowed upon return of the bottle.

Near Mrs. Whitlock's and next to The Brewery were The Lear Memorial Rooms belonging to St. Martin's Church. The entrance was through an iron gate some four feet in width — to the left was the caretaker's house and on the right a small committee room. The hall itself was on the far side of a courtyard which could not be built upon as it had been the burial ground of the Quakers in the eighteenth century. Further down the street was Young's Timber Yard having a narrow entrance under the bedrooms of adjoining houses which made deliveries difficult. The firm traded there for many years and a number of well-known craftsmen served their apprenticeships at the works.

It was quite amazing how many small shops existed in the 'twenties. Culver Street had three general stores, whilst in St. Ann's Street, the Post Office also sold stationery and sundries. On the other side of St. Ann's Street was another general store run by Mrs. Bryant, next to this came a greengrocery shop owned by her father-in-law. Old Mr. Bryant sold produce raised on three allotments in Bugmore rented from the City Council. Both Bryant families were strong Methodists and those who complain today about racism can have no idea of the gulf between Church and Chapel only seventy years ago.

Some fifty yards up the road beyond the greengrocers were two houses having front doorsteps about three feet above street level. The quite steep steps up to the doors took up almost half the pavement. In the second of these houses, next to a six foot wide snicket which led to Paynes Hill, lived the Burden family consisting, if memory serves, of father, mother and four or five children. Despite the number living in what was quite a small cottage, Mrs. Burden had turned the front room into a shop selling tobacco, confectionery and small oddments. How such a venture was ever worthwhile is debatable for it had the disadvantage of the steep climb from the pavement.

In the snicket only some three feet away from the wall of the shop was a public urinal, the dirtiest and smelliest I have every known. It was constructed of corrugated iron, with no roof and the running water system was seldom in working order.

At the top of St. Ann's Street at the Rampart Road corner was Mrs. Lanning's shop. This was never well stocked and could hardly have been a goldmine.

I've already mentioned the two general stores in Gigant Street, Whitlock's and Moody's, and just around the corner were two bakers, Naish's and Robbins', trading in Trinity Street. The first of these was rather spooky for there was little activity as Mr. Naish, a man in his sixties did all the work, baked the bread, then delivered this in a large wicker basket to his few remaining customers. He always looked tired and sad as he trudged along the streets. The shop certainly had not received a coat of paint in a long time and, though looking decrepit, in earlier years the well proportioned double-fronted premises must have been quite smart. Robbins, the other baker's shop, run by a widow with the help of her daughter, was quite different to Naish's for it was alive. Two bakers were employed, deliveries were made to all parts of the city and general goods were also sold. For some four years between 1922 and 1926, I was a member of the choir at The Trinity Hospital Chapel opposite Robbins'. We sang at the weekly service held at six o'clock each Thursday for the old gentlemen who were inmates of the hospital. If a Thursday coincided with a Saints Day, we were rewarded by being able to go across to Mrs. Robbins' after the service and order a pennyworth of sweets apiece — the Hospital trustees picking up the bill. Those treats were always a scrimmage — ten or twelve boys all endeavouring to be the first to catch Mrs. Robbins' eye.

There was a tiny shop at the Barnard's Cross — Love Lane corner, again just the front room of a cottage which belonged to Mr. Mont. Rattue who was a plumber. His mother-in-law ran the shop, such as it was, for she only sold soft drinks, firewood and her speciality — home made whiting balls. In those days many housewives still made their doorsteps shining white each morning.

Brown Street was almost devoid of shops. Mirfin's, near the Trinity Street corner was a small greengrocers and they had secondhand books as a side line. The only other shop was Hargreaves at the lower end of Brown Street between Trinity Street and St. Ann's Street — generally known as the posh end for it had a number of very large houses. In contrast Mr. Hargreaves' general stores was in a tiny cottage — again the front room had been adapted.

The area bordered by Brown Street, St. Ann's Street, Rampart Road and Milford Hill/Milford Street, each side measuring about 250 yards had eight General Stores, two Confectioners, two Greengrocers, one Newsagent and one Dairy serving a population of some fifteen hundred people.

To go shopping with my father and mother on Saturday evenings seemed quite an adventure, especially in the winter when, under the flickering gas lamps, Salisbury became a different city.

Most shops were open until eight o'clock; butchers and grocers closed at nine as did the market, lit in those days by oil lamps. Refrigeration was in its infancy, so that perishable goods just had to be sold which meant that prices were gradually reduced in the hour or so before closing time.

At that time, Butcher Row really was Butcher Row for it had no less than five, plus a fishmonger and a poulterer. The competition was intense and the shop managers would actually stand in the street touting for business. Mum had bought her meat from The British and Argentine Meat Company for many years and the buying of the Sunday joint was a regular Saturday ritual. Dad knew the manager quite well — Mr. Thomas, who lived in Waterloo Gardens. He would stand outside his window, which had a sloping marble slab, filled with joints carefully displayed in both horizontal and vertical rows. Mr. Thomas would enquire of the customers the exact requirement, take a quick look to find a suitable joint and signal to his assistant, Mr. Dimmer, who was stationed inside the shop. First of all he would indicate the vertical row, then tap on the window with a coin held between his fingers. One tap meant the bottom horizontal row, two the second row and so on. By the time the customer walked into the shop, the joint had been wrapped by a second assistant whilst a third would fill the empty space in the window. Even as a small boy, I admired the wonderfully simple system which enabled Mr. Thomas to sell a great deal of meat.

My mother usually required something from one or other of the drapers. There were so many of them — Style and Gerrish on The Blue Boar Row, Blooms on The Canal, Clarks at The Poultry Cross and Canal, David Stevens and Hobdens were both in Silver Street whilst Catherine Street was well endowed with Worleys, McIlroys and Fowler and Bailey. Fisherton Street also had two, Lords and Bon Marche whilst High Street housed Binghams. Hancock's triple-fronted shop was along Oatmeal Row in The Market Place and there were several one man bands in secondary positions. All had one thing in common, they were private concerns and also priced goods at $11^{3}/_{4}$ d, $1/11^{3}/_{4}$, $2/11^{3}/_{4}$ even $19/11^{3}/_{4}$. This draper's ploy was a bit of a con, for unless asked specifically for the farthing change, the assistant handed you a small card with perhaps three or four safety pins or a piece of paper with ordinary pins attached. The card or paper would say, "This is your change — thank you — please call again." I expect the draper made an extra $^1/_8$ penny on each transaction, not a fortune but could lead to one in a lifetime of trading.

Many of the shops, drapers especially, used an overhead railway system for the rapid giving of change. The assistant would write the bill, get it countersigned, take the money and put both into a small wooden cup which was then put into a socket on the overhead line. A swift turn of the wrist, a resulting click as the receptacle was locked, a pull on the lever and off it went to the central cash desk that usually had two cashiers. I used to spend all my time in these shops watching the cup speeding along the rail but never seeming to go to the wrong station. The quick service was quite fantastic and even chairs were provided for customers.

One of the busiest streets was Fisherton for hundreds of country people flocked into the City, taking advantage of the very economical Saturday tickets offered by the railway. Whenever I went to Fisherton Street it was a must for me to go to Pickfords, the carriers for The Great Western Railway, just to gaze in the window, for right in the centre was a beautiful scale model of one of their pantechnicons, some two feet in length. I am sorry to say that I often broke the tenth commandment for I really coveted that model and expect many of my contemporaries were also guilty of that sin.

On the corner of North Street was "The Toffee King", his two windows filled with tin trays, each holding a different sort of toffee. When you went into the shop to buy, he would take out a tray, give the toffee a tap with a small silver-plated hammer, put a fair size piece into the palm of his hand and tap away to produce chewable sized pieces. Gosh! that toffee was hard, took ages to chew and stuck to the teeth. Not to be recommended for those having a plate. His Brazil Nut slabs were especially good and it was a shame when the business closed in about 1930.

Nearly opposite The Toffee King was a tiny shop owned by a herbalist. I remember him running into trouble for selling medicines not labelled with the appropriate Patent Medicine Stamps — a form of taxation until the mid-'thirties. His excuse was forgetfulness but I expect the real reason was lack of funds.

Almost every Saturday, Dad wanted to go to Godwin's, the Leather Merchants who also sold Boots and Shoes. He had become quite friendly with the family — one brother ran the leather, the other the boot and shoe shop. I remember both as heavy smokers. Their father who had started the business, although retired, was still usually to be found there, hovering in the background, his full white beard reminding me of Father Christmas. A third son did, I believe, run a branch at Trowbridge.

Another of Dad's stopping places was the Magnet Stores, quite a large ironmongers with china and leather goods departments just below Godwin's on the same side of Fisherton Street. They also had an overhead railway which gave me unlimited pleasure and I well remember a wall covered with hundreds of tiny wooden drawers filled with different sizes of screws and nails. Outside the shop at first floor level was a magnificent six-foot magnet. I was not very old when Dad told me that if you stood under it for very long, it would attract the coins out of your pocket. Surreptitiously, I tried it, it didn't work, so I placed

Fisherton Street, c. 1915. The Magnet Stores are on the right with the giant magnet which did not pull the pennies from my pocket.

a coin on the palm of my hand, still it didn't work and I then discovered that the magnet was only made of wood.

There was a bazaar in Butcher Row belonging to The Arcadia Bazaar Company whilst round in Minster Street was one of the early ones owned by Marks and Spencer. Both establishments had open fronts so that conditions for employees could not have been pleasant during the winter months.

Opposite Marks and Spencers bazaar was an arcade providing a short cut through to The Market although it was always closed on Sundays, with locked gates at either end. On The Poultry Cross side of this was The Westminster Bank, on the other facing the Market, Singer Sewing Machines, and on the same side facing Minster Street, The London and Counties Clothing Company, a rather high sounding name for a not very large Men's Outfitters, owned and run by Mr. Selway who lived at the corner of Milford Hill/Rampart Road with his mother. After her death, he advertised for a housekeeper with a view to matrimony but unfortunately the first lady who took the job decamped after a few days, taking with her his prized possessions and helped by a male friend who apparently had kept in the background.

The Market on Saturday evenings provided much entertainment as always a number of cheapjacks were to be found selling all sorts of items. Cutlery wrapped in singed tissue paper as fire-salvaged stock. All types of medicines reputed to be the equal of branded goods except that generally they were just a load of rubbish. I recall the time that I saw on one of the stalls a bone-handled Scout knife and though only a Wolf-Cub, determined to buy one. The next Saturday, armed with my pocket money, I waited for about an hour before the cheap-jack came to the knives, which after a lot of spiel were offered for sixpence — all I possessed. Feeling as if I had just won a gold medal, I ran home, carefully examined my treasure to find that the "bone" handle was only painted tin. The salesmen's patter was good, polished at each performance and repeated daily as they attended different markets. Some were excellent comedians and would not have been out-of-place at The Palace Theatre.

One selling crockery could balance about six teaplates on one arm, a quick movement and they were in a neat pile in his hand. He also juggled three or four plates very professionally. Then there was a butcher, minus several bits of fingers, who would hold up his hand and joke,

"You won't find 'em in the sausages, missus."

The local man who comes to mind is Mr. Len Cannell who sold fruit. He would blow into one of his paper bags, somehow or another keep this in position, still open on his left hand and then with his right throw oranges into it. He would count,

"One, two, three, four, five, six, let's have some apples — one, two, three, four, five, six, now what about some bananas,"

And a bunch would be added.

"Now who's going to give me half-a-crown — go on then two bob — what's the matter with you all — alright then one and six! Lady over there."

Then Mr. Cannell repeated the process meanwhile providing first-class free entertainment for onlookers who had no intention of buying anything.

A shop that fascinated me as a youngster was Wrides, towards the Ivy Street end of Catherine Street. Between about 1922 and 1925 they sold Army Surplus tools and oddments of which there were a great deal at the end of World War I, obtainable at give away prices. After joining the Wolf Cubs, my first billy-can was purchased at Wrides for only 6d. Brand new — in first class condition it must have cost many times that to make, being in heavy tin and having a lid with collapsible handle that turned it into a frying pan. They also sold rubber gas mask tubing which was corrugated and covered in heavy canvas. Originally about a foot long, it had been cut into two, when they made excellent cycle handlebar grips for only 3d a pair. Wrides also had examples of turning swords into ploughshares for bayonets had been hinged into notched steel bases for sale as very effective firewood splitters. However, on the one occasion that I bought fretsaw blades from them for 3d a dozen, a penny cheaper than elsewhere, I found that they were very inferior, breaking almost immediately.

A shop that had an annual visit from me was Higgins the Chemists in Blue Boar Row, for I was sent there regularly on Boxing Day. This was always "the morning after the day before" for Dad who used to eat much more than usual on Christmas Day and the nuts that he consumed, plus the unaccustomed glass or two of Cripp's Tarragona wine all went to help upset his tummy. Higgins always opened each Boxing Day morning and I was dispatched to buy their own brand of

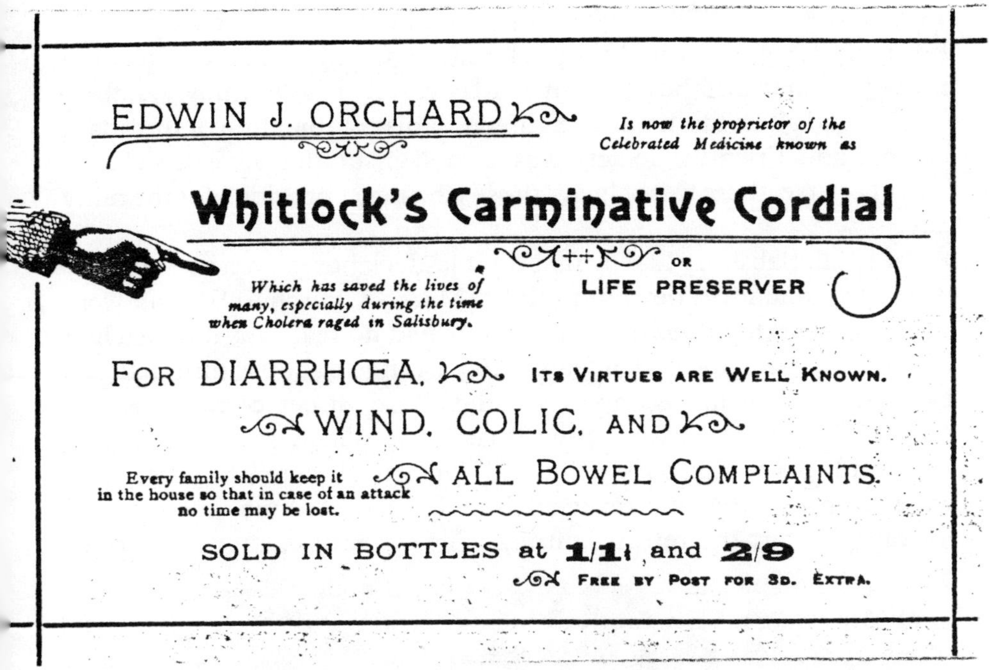

This Victorian advertisement claims that Carminative Cordial (in which Dad had so much faith) "saved the lives of many, especially during the time when cholera raged in Salisbury" (1849). Edwin J. Orchard's Chemists shop in Blue Boar Row was sold to C.N.Higgins just before the Great War.

"Carminative Cordial". This usually put Dad to rights but must have been pretty potent stuff as it ceased to be available after the war.

Should there be a diptheria outbreak in the surrounding streets, one or other of us would be sent for a bottle of Fennings Fever Curer, either from Higgins or Newtons, the Catherine Street Chemists. Made by Alfred Fennings at Cowes on the Isle of Wight, this again was fairly strong, vile liquid to swallow but most effective. I remember that after being dosed with the concoction — your mouth was dry for hours afterwards. I believe its main ingredient was quinine and doubt if it can be obtained today.

Before the advent of the National Health Service in 1948, prudent people belonged to the Infirmary League and one or other of the sick clubs run by Friendly Societies such as The Ancient Order of Foresters,

The Oddfellows, The Rechabites and The National Deposit. The Infirmary League covered hospital treatment and cost 2d a week for a single person whilst the payment of 4d covered a whole family — father, mother and all children under eighteen. This combination of Infirmary League and Friendly Society was a good insurance against sickness but, of course, there were always those who never provided for the rainy day.

In 1920, Salisbury had its first double-deck buses even though they were secondhand. They ran from St. Mark's Church to Wilton, were open tops and the poor drivers not only had no real cabs but also had to share their outside bench seats with passengers at busy times. In the early years until the Rampart Road/Milford Street corner was improved the route was from Blue Boar Row, Winchester Street along London Road to St. Mark's Church. On arrival there, the passengers were dropped, the bus reversed into Bourne Avenue, then pulled forward to start the return journey. A few months after the service

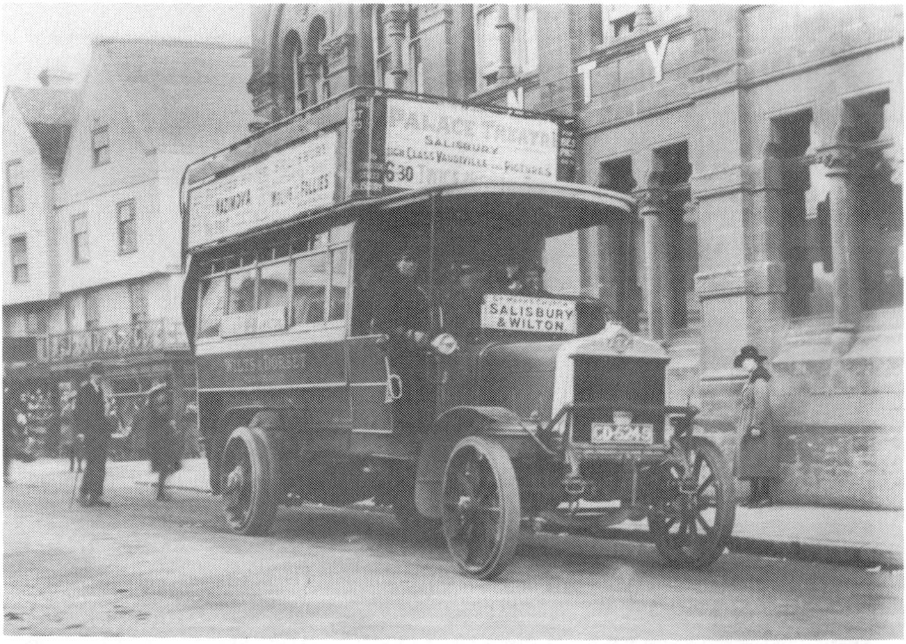

One of the first open-top Wilts and Dorset buses outside The County Hotel in Bridge Street, 1920.

started there was a tragedy when the young daughter of Mr. Whitehead, Headmaster of The Salisbury School (now Chafyn Grove) was killed as she ran behind the reversing bus from which she had just alighted.

As they came back into the City, buses had to slow almost to a halt to safely make the turn into Winchester Street; it was not only steep but also had a tricky camber.

My first ride on a double-deck, on the open top of course, was from Bridge Street corner, outside The County Hotel to The Nelson Hotel near the Railway Bridge at the top end of Fisherton Street. The occasion was the purchase of a new carpenter's apron for my father and Mum said that as a special treat, my two sisters and I could travel on the bus, one way. This was only a week after the start of what was almost a revolutionary service — the cost: 1d for my eldest sister who was fourteen and half price or $^1/_2$d for my other sister and myself.

Double-deckers remained open-top almost throughout that decade, the first roofed vehicles appearing in 1929.

8 *Murder*

On a Monday morning, early in 1921, Salisbury was buzzing with the news of the murder of a local taxi-driver. I wonder why things always happened on a Monday, but it seemed to be the case.

As I remember, Mr. Sidney Spicer drove a taxi, having some connection with Rogers Garage in London Road. He had picked up a fare in the City — an army deserter called Percy Toplis, who asked to be driven to Basingstoke. On the way, just before Andover, he shot Spicer in the back of the head and as a result was on the run from police for several weeks.

That Monday, for some reason, my sisters and I were despatched to Fair View Road where Uncle Ernest, Dad's brother, lived with his second wife, Aunt Ella. On the way, all my sisters talked about was the murder and when, on reaching the corner of Fair View Road and Kelsey Road, we met my cousin Violet the gossip was renewed with interest.

The gardens of the Manor Road houses went through to one side of Fair View Road and my cousin pointed out a Nissen Hut in one of them as the garage rented by Mr. Rogers where the fateful taxi had been kept. I looked at the double doors in horror and wondered if perchance Toplis might be hiding inside. Every time that I passed the spot, over the next year or two, I glanced quickly at the building, then scooted past.

Toplis was eventually cornered by police, I believe in Cumberland, and the murderer was shot dead whilst resisting arrest.

On Christmas Day, 1921, all the family went to Uncle Ern's to tea. I was fascinated by a large, framed print on the wall, depicting a tragedy that occurred in the Mediterranean around the turn of the century. The picture was called "The Sinking of the Camperdown". I wonder why people hung this sort of thing on the wall to be looked at day after day. Apparently the Mediterranean Fleet, on exercises, were steaming in two parallel lines some three-quarters of a mile apart. Admiral of the Fleet, Lord Tryon, gave the order for the lines to circle inwards towards one another and, after completing a turn of 180 degrees, steam in the reverse direction. His officers were aghast, pointing out that the minimum turning circle was half a mile and did their best to dissuade him. All to no avail, the Admiral saying that if his instructions were obeyed, the ships would pass over the centre line alternately. What he obviously had in mind was the manoeuvre carried out by horsemen displaying their skill at a gymkhana. To carry out the same thing with battleships was a very different matter and the collision the officers had foreseen duly occurred. *The Camperdown* was cut in half — sank quickly with a resulting loss of the lives of over one thousand men including the stubborn Admiral.

During the evening of that Christmas Day came a really bright spot as far as I was concerned. Uncle Ern said to my cousin Jim who was some six years older than me, "Why don't you go and get that old box of fag cards for Arthur." This he did and later in the evening he said that I could keep them. At this time none of the tobacco companies had issued cards since early in the war, so this shoe box, mostly full of sets, was indeed a treasure. It contained amongst others a set of "Flags of all Nations", each one about two inches square and printed on white silk. The cigarette companies started to issue cards once again in the middle of 1922 and they quickly became a craze.

Among the first sets were "Cries of London" from John Player (a set of 25), "Do You Know?" from W.D. & H.O. Wills (a set of 50) and even the smaller firm of Ansties at Devizes came up with "Racehorse Owners and their Colours". This again was a set of 25 — I collected twenty-four different ones but was short of Lord Woolavington and this one was really scarce. Eventually Jim Humby who was in Standard Two at school (I was in one at this time) told me that he had a spare. This was when I learnt for the first time how experts conducted dealing for Jim came from a family of dealers. He taught me the lesson of supply and demand for, although quite willing to swap, he demanded twelve of my Anstie spares for the one card. My pleas fell upon deaf ears — that was the deal, I could take it or leave it. I wanted that card to complete the set, so ruefully handed over twelve of my duplicates. The "Do You Know?" set issued by Wills was very instructive and I for one learnt many little known facts from them, including the origin of the Sargasso Sea.

Fag cards became a game that was very popular, for this only common changers were used. Two or more could play and a coin (if you possessed one) was tossed for the first to throw. You stood in the gutter, on the edge of the pavement, held the corner of a card between the first and second fingers of the right hand and flicked. If you were skilled the card flew to the back of the pavement and the next player threw, trying to cover the first card with his. Sometimes there would be two hundred cards on the pavement before someone fluked a cover and then all the cards were his and he cleared the deck. There were all sorts of minor wins, for instance if you threw and your card laid perfectly along the edge of another without covering it, that was a "touchee". There was a great deal of noise and the shouts of "Cover!" and "Touchee!" were as loud as any Australian Test Team appealing for L.B.W. and often with the same lack of justification. Needless to say a great deal of cheating occurred — the biggest boy's interpretation of the rules having to be accepted unless you were brave enough to risk a good hiding.

For a few weeks each autumn, conkers was the game in vogue. We used to take a basket and trudge over a mile to a huge horse chestnut tree that grew just past Petersfinger on the Southampton Road, its branches stretching right across from side to side. Usually we found enough conkers for our needs already on the ground, but if this was not the case, then a few well aimed throws with sticks would soon bring more ripe fruits cascading down. Then home we would go and share out the proceeds from our trip. Then our mothers would be prevailed upon to loan metal meat skewers with which to bore holes in the centres of the conkers. More scrounging for good, strong but not thick string, a quick knot, the string was threaded through the conker and you were ready to do battle. You tossed your opponent for first strike, then the loser just stood still like a lemon with his conker dangling from the string. Standing still was important for if the conker was swaying about, the striker had a free go.

The winner of the toss usually wound his string around his hand except for the last six inches, this ensured a good sharp and hard blow on the other conker. A miss meant the opponent took over. Should the strings become entwined then the first protagonist to shout

"Strings!" had strike and so the conker bashing went on until one split. The winner's conker was then a oner, when it had disposed of two it became a twoer, but if it should then beat a threeer it then became a fiver. Strange logic but that was the rule. All sorts of tricks were tried in order to harden the conkers — gentle baking, soaking in a mixture of salt and vinegar, but I think the best way was to allow them to harden naturally in the sun on a window sill. The largest conkers seldom made the toughest, it was often smaller ones about an inch across which attained astronomical figures, calculated by means of the strange method used for scoring. Most important of all was to have a good aim using a short string as this would produce telling hits, quickly demolishing the opponent's conker.

Two other games, now no more than a memory, were tops and hoops. Both were winter occupations and helped keep you warm on a cold day. There were two sorts of tops — "spinners" and "window breakers" both costing tuppence. Spinners were of a short, fat, carrot-like shape, turned in hardwood with a coned-shape metal stud in the centre of the base on which the top spun. "Window breakers" were T-shaped, rather like a tall toadstool. The method used to spin both types was the same, a short whip of string or leather about eighteen inches in length was wound around the top which was then placed upright on the ground and steadied with one finger. A sharp pull on the whip and with luck it would spin. From then on you whipped every time the top slowed down, the "spinners" would generally move up to two feet, then carry on turning with increased speed. The "window breakers", as their name implies would sometimes fly ten or twenty feet making their use most unpopular with our elders.

Another game requiring a deal of skill was "Tip-E-Cat". This was played with a piece of wood about six inches in length and three quarters of an inch in diameter, sharpened to a point at both ends and then placed on the ground. With a stick some eighteen inches long, you gave the first stick a tap at the point causing it to spring in the air. Whilst it was still airborne you gave it an almighty swipe and endeavoured to send it further than your opponent. Sometimes, but not too often, there was the sound of a window being broken, whereupon a general speedy exodus took place, with the consequent panic whenever a knock came at the street door during the next few days.

Hoops used to be brought out from time to time, to become a craze, then be forgotten again. It only wanted one to make an appearance and out they came. Some children were quite expert with wooden hoops guided by a short stick. However, as befitted the son of a coachsmith, I had one made from quarter inch round steel and guided by a steel crook fitted into a wooden handle. About four feet in diameter, it really was a beauty and always being borrowed by my friends, something I never objected to, for the hoop was virtually unbreakable. We all became experts and could perform quite a number of tricky manoeuvres. One of the great advantages that we had in the 'twenties was comparatively safe and clear streets, parked cars would have stopped many of our games and I imagine that tops would not have been popular with car owners.

These days you hardly ever see a child with a small rubber or tennis ball. We were never without one for even when your friends were unavailable, it was still possible to have splendid games just bouncing the ball against a wall and catching it, something that gave hours of pleasure and, what was more important, trained the eye. Some of the ball games played by girls were especially difficult. They would throw the ball against a wall, do one or more twirls and still have time to catch when it came down. The females also favoured games like hopscotch with the lines being chalked on the pavements — something that I'm sure would be frowned on today. Most girls seemed to spend hours skipping away without getting tired.

From time to time, one or other of the local shops would display marbles in their window, producing a sudden craze for the game. They were cheap to buy, somewhere I believe at about ten for a penny. In fact all the games mentioned were inexpensive, they had to be, few people had spare cash for inessentials. We had just as much fun from them, perhaps even more, than modern children have with toys costing a small fortune.

Dad was a wonderful craftsman and created many toys from scrap. When I was about four years of age, he made a working model roundabout with galloping horses. As the roundabout was pulled along it revolved and it was a shame that the lead horses used as the gallopers were so brittle. The toy that I remember lasting for quite a long time was a beautifully made wooden engine with its tender and two trucks. The boiler and wheels were hand-turned by Mr. Player of Milford Street. The train was large enough to carry one boy on the engine, with one in each truck. It was pulled along by a rope at the front and when loaded with its full complement of three, required two boys to do the pulling along the pavement. Needless to say, frequent arguments broke out as to whose turn it was to ride or pull. The train was substantially made of strong timber and my father had painted it green — the livery colour of the London and South Western Railway.

One morning, early in 1923, Dad came home to breakfast, carrying what appeared to be old ironwork. It was in fact the back axle of a lady's tricycle which he had seen laying discarded on the top of someone's dustbin. Mum asked what he wanted it for and he just said, "I've got an idea". What an idea! A few months later that piece of old scrap had become the basis of a mainly timber-built, chain-driven model motor car, on the lines of the bull-nosed Morris Cowley with a rounded back. The steering was both ingenious and strong and again Mr. Player was called upon, on this occasion to provide the steering wheel. The car must have been exceptionally sturdy for it often had me driving and pedalling like mad, with one friend perched on the bonnet and another on the back. Braking was by means of the fixed gear transmission and an emergency stop could mean bashed knees as they were forced up against the dashboard and steering wheel. A few years later, mass produced model cars were commonplace, but thanks to Dad my friends and I spent many happy hours with the early version he produced in 1923.

Later during that same year, my father came home to say that a friend had a bike for sale. It was too large for me at that time, but over the next twelve months I must have grown considerably because, with wooden blocks fixed on the pedals, I was able to reach it in comparative comfort. The machine cost two pounds and the purchase took all the money from my Post Office Savings plus three shillings which Mum, Dad and the ever generous Aunt Gertrude produced. My one pound, seventeen shillings had been put together over a number of years by saving money given me on my birthdays by relatives. Once I had learnt to ride, the trick of balancing took me quite a while, that bike, over the next four years gave me enormous pleasure. Traffic was light in those days and I explored South Wiltshire — in fact the whole area some fifteen miles around Salisbury. On one, never to be forgotten occasion, I went to Stonehenge, had a puncture after only a mile on the way back and then had to walk nine miles home. My friend went on ahead and told Mum what had happened and Dad, after leaving work, came out to meet me. By the time we met I had almost reached The Old Castle Inn at Old Sarum and good old Dad bought me the largest ginger beer I've ever had. That episode made me quickly learn how to repair a puncture and from that time on I always carried a repair outfit.

In June 1925, we had a school holiday on a Wednesday, so with a schoolmate set off to ride to Ringwood. The journey there was uneventful and we sat on a seat in the Market Place to eat our sandwiches. On the way back we were about two and a half miles from Fordingbridge when disaster struck. The nut and bolt holding my friend's chain came off and there we were, two ten-year-olds, some fourteen miles from home with a useless bike. We could see the village of Ibsley off to our right so down a side road we trudged and found a cycle repairer — almost every village had one. There was one snag however — we had no money, a fact which really did worry me. Alf, my friend asked the man if he could mend the chain and within ten minutes it was done. They he said, "That'll cost ee fourpence". Only then to my embarrassment did Alf tell him of our predicament. The chap grinned,

"Where do ee live?"

"Salisbury."

"Well you'll have to bring it back out to me, won't ee?"

We thanked him and cycled back home without further mishap. On many occasions I asked Alf if he had taken the money to pay the debt but he never did! I felt that it was pretty rotten after the way the chap helped us, especially as my friend came from a staunch Church family.

9 *Uncle Fred, or a Runaway Makes Good!*

Early in 1923, Dad had to go hurriedly to Devon to attend the funeral of one of his elder brothers, Uncle Fred, who had died as the result of a heart attack at the early age of forty-seven.

Only two years previously, my uncle had been accepted as a coastguard and took up his position at Babbacombe, near Torquay, after almost thirty years' service as a Royal Marine. The coastguard cottages had a splendid view overlooking Torbay. Uncle Fred left four sons, two of whom had followed him into the Marines and a widow, Aunt May, who suffered from what was then referred to as shaking palsy.

The coastguard duties included patrolling paths at the top of high and sheer cliffs — not a job for the faint-hearted. Uncle Fred had become a marine because of rather unusual circumstances.

Dad's family were living at Charlton-All-Saints between Salisbury and Downton in the mid eighteen-nineties and, as was the custom, not only grandfather but also his two elder sons were working on the same farm. Grandfather's wage was the magnificent sum of twelve shillings per week and of course he lived in a tied cottage. Although Dad was still at school, he also had to help. One of his jobs after school was to collect some of the farm horses and lead them back to stables in the farmyard. One evening, he was probably either tired or feeling very daring for he decided to ride and entered the yard in style, unfortunately being spotted by the farmer who started to use his horsewhip on the small boy. The incident was witnessed by Uncle Fred, a well built lad of eighteen, who happened to be working with a pitchfork nearby. This he promptly brought into action in defence of his small brother, ran the farmer against a wall and threatened to run the fork through the aggressor. Fortunately other workers were near enough to restrain Uncle Fred before he had time to carry out his threat, with the result that a badly shaken farmer went off into the farmhouse, saying that he would fetch the police in the morning — no telephones in those days. The delay gave Uncle Fred breathing space, so he packed a few things, walked the four miles into Salisbury, caught the train to Portsmouth and joined the Marines. The farmer, thwarted in his desire to punish Uncle Fred, then vented his spite on Grandfather and the rest of the family. They had to leave their cottage within a week but fortunately another job with a cottage was obtained in Downton.

When I was small, Uncle Fred was my hero and I listened in awe as he told Dad of some of his experiences as a Marine. He had seen service in the Boer War and the Boxer Rebellion of 1900 in China before service on the Royal Yacht during King Edward VII's reign. I remember him telling Dad that he was on duty outside the King's Cabin Door when "the dirty old devil was inside with one of his fancy ladies." Although remembered, at the time, I had no idea what Uncle Fred was on about. He was serving on the battleship *HMS Agincourt* during the Battle of Jutland and related how they were in line astern to *The Queen Mary* and, when the latter was hit in the magazine and blew up, they sailed over the spot without feeling a thing. These tales made quite an impression on me as did the story of Uncle Fred's eldest son, young Fred as he was known, putting on his age and managing to join the Marines when only sixteen, then found himself serving on the same ship as his father during the great battle — something of a unique record. After the war, young Fred did a spell of duty in the Far East, mainly Hong Kong, where he became a member of the Marine Band. According to Dad he was quite wild — on returning to this country (he was still hardly twenty) — not surprising after his experiences.

He went to Poole, where my Aunt and her family lived and, on one occasion walked down the High Street wearing Chinese garb and sporting a pigtail. Imagine my poor Aunt's reaction when told by a shocked neighbour that her eldest daughter was walking out with a Chinaman. He stayed with us for a while in Salisbury early in 1921 and I can still hear him thumping away on the piano singing his favourite song "Signora" in a not very tuneful voice. He pronounced it "Sig-Nora", not having the benefit of correct pronunciation via the radio or television. Each evening he was off to the local pub The Royal Oak where he apparently became the life and soul of the party. Not only did he treat everyone in sight but also led nightly singsongs by thumping away on the pub piano. The treating, perhaps fortunately, cut his visit short for after a few nights of festivities he was stoney broke. So stoney that he even had to borrow money from Dad to get home. I say borrow but the cash was never refunded and I expect Dad thought it was a cheap way to get rid of him. It was strange that this wild young man settled down to an exemplary career as a Marine and on retirement became a probation officer. Fred's younger brother Sid also became a marine and both were bandsmen for many years!

A story which I heard from Dad about his days at Charlton-All-Saints brought a chuckle from him as he told it but, at the time, the occasion must have been almost tragic. As with all farm workers during the last century, Dad's family were used to poverty — never any sweets or treats and barely enough money to exist. Grandmother Maidment was a good manager, a good cook who could make a meal out of nothing and was especially expert with currant duff, steamed suet pudding made in a cloth. One morning a carter and his son were delivering a load of firewood and Grandmother asked if they would like a slice of pudding before they left. The carter said "Yes, please", so Grandmother put the pudding on a plate, placed it on the table, whereupon the carter said "Me and the boy likes the ends". Grandmother said, "There's a knife — help yourself". To the horror of the watching children he just sliced the pudding in half — gave one piece to his son and quickly devoured the rest. It must have been a terrible experience to see the meal vanish before their eyes — one that Dad never forgot.

10 *Farr's — Coach-Builders of Brown Street*

From the time that I was about four, each fine weekday evening during the summer months, I trotted off to meet my father from his work at Farrs, the Coachbuilders in Brown Street. Dad was the coachsmith, a highly skilled trade and in the eyes of his contemporaries (as I learned from them in later life) he was an excellent craftsman.

I was instructed not to be too early — to wait quietly outside the entrance and not make a nuisance of myself. The thought occurs to me — there I was only four, yet going on my own some five hundred yards, having to cross a road, yet all in perfect safety. At that time, there was no thought of child molesters — how different to the present day.

It was not long before Mrs. Farr used to look out for me, I would be invited in, a slice of cake was waiting and Bess, the black spaniel, would be fussing around, licking my knees. She was the first dog that I got to know and I've been a sucker for them ever since.

One evening as I was nearing Farr's entrance, I was running, tripped, with the result that I banged my head on the pavement. Mrs. Farr, hearing my screams, came out, picked me up, carried me into the house, calmed me down, then applied some first aid. A large cold knife was held to my forehead, to bring out the bruise, then butter was applied. Dad was called, a discussion ensued whether the doctor should look at the bump, the size of a pigeon's egg, that had appeared. Should the wound be stitched? All very frightening to a small boy wondering if he would die. Sweets were produced and I remember going around with a bandaged head for a day or so.

Farrs fronted Brown Street; on the left hand side were the sliding glass doors to the showroom, just large enough to take one vehicle. To the right were double doors, one three feet wide, the other about six feet in width was only opened for the movement of vehicles. Behind the showroom was the Farrs' house which on the first floor extended to the street. There was a sizeable yard at the rear of the house and in front of the works, which had large double doors at both ground and first floor level. The upper storey covered only the left hand side of the ground floor and it was up there that vehicle bodies took shape. To the right on the ground floor were the carpenter's benches whilst the area to the left, under the first floor housed the machinery, mainly woodworking but also drills, grindstones and a guillotine for chopping steel bars into lengths. All the machinery was powered by a gas engine which drove a long shaft near the ceiling that in turn, by means of belts to fast and loose pulleys, provided the motive power for the various equipment. I can still remember the slapping of the leather belts against the pulleys and the almost firework display as sparks flew when steel was being shaped on a grindstone.

The carpenter's benches were well lit by roof lights; some of the tools used at that time would probably not be found today. Tools such as

The staff at Farrs' in 1912. Mr Frank Farr is third from the left in the back row. My father is seated, second from the left and others in the group include Arthur Kingshott, Sid White, Jack Adlam, George Searle, Billy Feltham, Harry Acton and Arthur Rolfe.

bow saws, spokeshaves and routing planes required for jobs that electric equivalents do so much more easily now. The only way up to the first floor from inside the works was via a ladder, which had started life as one of The Salisbury Volunteer Fire Brigade escapes, probably acquired by Mr. Farr during his service as a fireman in the early years of the century. It still wore its fire-engine red livery. Looking back, one can only wonder why no-one suggested easier ways of working, great economies could have been made if a time and motion expert had been employed. Instead it meant hard work with a capital H for all the fifteen or so staff.

Up in the top shop, the vehicle bodies, usually charabancs, carrier's buses or delivery vehicles were constructed on two six-inch by four inch baulks of timber. The woods most used in construction were elm and ash, both very hard and durable. The skeleton of the body took shape and when complete would be lifted on to rollers, rolled along the timber, out through the double doors and down to the waiting chassis in the yard by means of skids. A pulley block was used to ensure the safety of this manoeuvre. I have no idea why the body could not have been built directly onto the chassis at ground level for so much effort would have been saved. There must have been a good reason for the same method was also in use at other coach works. The ironwork was now fitted and the chassis with its partly constructed body was taken some four hundred yards down the road into Farr's Friary Lane Works where panels, seats, hoods and fittings were added. Finally it was taken into the adjoining paint shop where the painting was done by hand, a laborious task. The paint was brushed on, rubbed down, another coat, another rub, until perhaps ten or twelve coats had been applied to give what can only be described as a wonderful finish. All the craftsmen took a real pride in their work, receiving only one shilling and threepence an hour but still realising how much better off they were than previous generations.

The smith's shop where my father worked was reached through a doorway at the right of the carpenter's shop. It was on a lower level than the rest of the works and was lit by windows which ran the length of the wall facing the doorway. A bench made of timber some three inches in thickness filled the space under the window. At either end of this, a heavy duty vice having jaws about eight or nine inches in length.

To the left of the doorway was the brick-built forge with a bed, some four feet square, having a pyramid-shaped chimney at the head. The bellows were operated by a handle that had to be turned slowly and regularly to ensure a good even fire. At the bottom of the forge was a water trough whilst some two feet in front of this stood the anvil, on a base cut from an elm trunk some three feet in diameter and two in height. The wall to the right of the door was covered with tools of the trade — chisels and punches of every size, mostly with handles of twisted willow which allowed the smith to hold them whilst they were struck with a seven pound sledgehammer and feel no vibration. On the floor was a large flat sheet of steel on which patterns were drawn in chalk. For instance, if a leaf spring was being made, each leaf would be tested against the pattern whilst work proceeded to ensure the correct curve. All this whilst the steel was still hot. On another part of the floor was a circular steel plate with a hole in the centre. This was used for the fitting of steel tyres to cartwheels. The newly made wooden wheel— the hub of elm, the spokes and rim of ash — was laid on the plate, the hub fitting snugly into the centre hole. The red-hot steel tyre would be placed in position around the wheel; if the tyre was of less width than the rim, temporary nails were partly driven into the wood to stop the tyre slipping down to the steel plate. It usually took two men to hold the tyre and if the smith thought the fit was satisfactory — at this time it was half-an-inch larger than the wheel — the boy helping was ordered to throw buckets of cold water over the still very hot steel which would immediately contract and tightly hold the rim. Then several fixing screws would be driven through ready-prepared counter-sunk holes in the tyre to ensure that never throughout a long life would it be able to slip. It was not unusual for a well made wheel to last fifty years or more; centuries of know-how were built into each one.

The fire in the forge was kept going from Monday morning through to next week-end. Overnight it was damped down, covered with coal dust and the next morning a few turns with the bellows handle would have it ready for the day's work. The fuel used was carefully chosen — hard Welsh nuts only about the size of marbles. When steel was being tempered, hazel twigs were used to test the metal's heat, the stick about a foot long was rubbed on the steel. If it smouldered quickly but did not burst into flame, the temperature was judged to be right — an archaic method that worked. Dad used to get his hazel twigs from a forester at Winterslow who knew exactly when they should be cut.

Sledgehammers were usually wielded by the apprentice; it was hot and heavy work. I remember one lad, Nobby Clark, who could not stand the pace. Both he and another old St. Martin's boy, Spud Hayter, started at Farr's the same week, Spud in the Carpenter's shop. One morning when the staff were sat down eating sandwiches, the clock at the adjoining Trinity Hospital chimed the hour, although it hardly chimed — it clanked. Someone, a bit of a wag, said, "Time they had a new stick to hit that there bell." Another said, "Why don't Spud and Nobby make 'em one — it'll be good practice for 'em." Poor Spud spent hours rounding a length of wood, which despite his herculean efforts was never smooth enough to satisfy his tormentors. In the meantime, Nobby was engaged in fashioning a piece of metal to fit over the top of the stick. At last, their mentors were satisfied, the implement was gift-wrapped and the two fourteen year olds despatched to present it to the Matron of Trinity Hospital. Poor kids, but in those days youngsters had their wits quickly sharpened by such antics.

The coachbuilding trade employees were paid by the hour and only one hour's notice was needed to either terminate employment or vary the hours to be worked. Contracts of employment were unknown and I remember the gloom at home if Dad announced that the works were going on to short time. No pay was given for Bank Holidays, with the result that it took weeks to recover from the loss of income. A man might be sacked at an hour's notice, perhaps after giving years of service, yet received no compensation, no redundancy payment. Although conditions had improved since Dickens' day, "hard times" were still prevalent.

Mr. Frank Farr leased a garden at the end of a lane called Prospect Place, the entrance being between The Saint Ann's Street Post Office and Hibberds Antique Shop. The first floor of the Post Office had some rooms over the lane which contained at the end nearest the street, some of Salisbury's oldest buildings. Hibberds workshops behind the shop were beautifully timbered, not a straight line to be seen anywhere, whilst the Post Office buildings, including an old bakehouse, appeared to be of the same period.

During the early summer of 1920, a bakers' strike led to Dad's lifelong friend, Walter Shipsey, leaving the employ of Suttons, the High Street Bakers, leasing the bakery in Prospect Place and launching into business in partnership with a Mr. Sheppard. The two men were quite different characters: Shipsey, the baker — very hard working, a cheerful, outgoing individual, whilst his partner — Sheppard — was a doleful looking man with a droopy moustache. He did however, have a fateful attraction for some of the ladies as he delivered the bread, for as a result the partnership of Shipsey and Sheppard lasted only a few years.

Dad used to sometimes work in Mr. Farr's garden on Saturday afternoons and would take me along with him. One such trip was during the first week that Mr. Shipsey started his business — the bakery door was open and Dad and I stood and watched the proceedings, I gazed in amazement as the tin loaves were drawn from the oven, trays of currant buns brought out, brushed with sugar water applied by a three inch brush and doughnuts sprinkled with sugar. It was a wonderful experience for a small boy and seventy years later the lovely smell of the warm bakehouse is well remembered. From this small beginning, Mr. Shipsey went on to greater things for we used to hear of his progress after the monthly meetings of the Ancient Order of Foresters as both Dad and his friend were Past Chief Rangers. I am glad that the business continues to flourish in the capable hands of Rodney Shipsey — the third generation.

Just further down the lane were three tiny cottages which always looked spruce in this quiet backwater and their small gardens were bright with flowers. Mr. Farr's garden was on the right hand side at the end of the footpath and must have been almost an acre in extent. Just inside the gate was a tool shed having a well with no wall around it. Right from the start, Dad told me never, ever, to go near it as if I fell in, I would most certainly drown. This warning whetted my appetite for I used to crawl to the edge and look down at the water which was usually quite near the top as this part of the city is barely above river level. I was also warned to stay away from the tennis court if anyone was playing, but on one Saturday, a party was in progress and Miss Betty Farr, who must have been in her early twenties, spotted me trying not to be seen, called me over and plied me with cakes and lemonade.

At one time, the apple trees were proving a great temptation to young men who would shin over the wall at night. Dad and Mr. Farr had a consultation on preventive measures. As a result my father collected sacks of old glass bottles and put a strong mixture of sand and cement on top of the wall. He then broke the bottles and stuck pieces

My father in the garden at home with my first dog Nip who tore poor Bess to pieces.

in the mortar. This array of jagged glass deterred the marauders, for the scrumping ceased.

Mr. Farr's dog Bess was often with him when he went to the garden and we were good friends, having wonderful games of hide and seek. I would hide stones and Bess would rout round with her nose, never giving up until they were found. In 1922 she was put down. I just thought at that time she had died, for that was what they told me. Mr. Farr then had her stuffed and gave poor Bess to me. She stayed under a side table in the front room until in 1925 my own dog "Nip", a terrier, took a dislike to this strange animal with glaring eyes and proceeded to tear her to pieces.

To supplement the low incomes of the 'twenties, there was a plentiful supply of Salisbury Corporation allotments for those with energy to work them. Although the average working week was still forty-eight hours, most men at that time had been reared when toil used to start at six o'clock in the morning and carried on until eight each evening. Neither did they have the distractions of radio or television, so an evening spent gardening in the open air was a worthwhile relaxation.

My father had his allotment at Bugmore and felt himself fortunate, for prior to becoming gardens the area had been filter beds for the City's Sewage Works. It was thus well manured and amply repaid any work spent on it. His twenty-rod patch cost him twelve shillings a year in rent and produced not only sufficient potatoes to feed the family from late May round to April the following year, but also a variety of other vegetables. He always found room for a long line of sweet peas; it gave him immense pleasure to pick an armful of these, take them home, present them to Mum and fill the house with their glorious scent.

I was about five when Dad started taking me with him when he went off to the allotment and I remember how, on a Wednesday evening, we went to Johnny Lampard's yard in Exeter Street. Johnny was an old friend of my father's and as a carrier still had a number of horse-drawn carts in addition to his expanding fleet of ex-Army lorries. Dad spent quite a time loading manure on to a flat-bedded cart, harnessed a horse, put it between the shafts and away to Bugmore we went, with me feeling like a king beside him. I had no idea that Dad could drive a horse, but this he did in great style for of course he had spent his boyhood on various farms.

Each Good Friday was earmarked by most men as potato-planting day at the allotments. I was sent to The Children's Service, usually held at St. Mary Magdalene's Church in Gigant Street at 9.30 am. We always sang "There is a green hill far away, without a City wall" and when small, I thought that "without" really meant that the green hill was minus a wall. We came out from church at about quarter-past ten and I would scoot home, for it was my job to take a can of tea and hot-cross buns (they were really hot) down to Dad already hard at work in the allotment. Armed with this treat, I ran most of the way to Bugmore, where Dad would stop work, off we would go to the shed, sit on the upturned wooden wheelbarrow and thoroughly enjoy the snack. Nothing ever tasted better than those lovely juicy, spicey buns filled with lots of fruit. As for the shed, it was in reality the body from an old motor-van, for on the sides, even though an attempt had been made to obliterate it, was the legend, "H. Martin and Sons, Mineral Water Manufacturers, Castle Street, Salisbury." Obviously at some time in the past, Farrs had put a new body on the chassis and Dad had seen the possibilities of the old one as an allotment shed. Even though it was open at the front and was full of gardening tools, nothing was ever stolen.

One of the problems with allotment gardening at Bugmore on Good Friday was the necessity to dodge the congregations; on their way to church at St. Martin's they would pass Bugmore Lane, the only way into the gardens. Dad was a regular churchgoer himself, a sidesman, so it just would not do for him to be seen working on such a special day in the Church Calendar. In the twenties, many more people attended church and the highlight of Good Friday was the Three Hour Service of Devotion, starting at midday and finishing at three o'clock, although few of the congregation remained right throughout the service. At one o'clock a hymn was sung to enable those wishing to leave to do so whilst newcomers entered. The same procedure was followed at two o'clock. The top of Bugmore Lane was only a hundred yards from the Church, so gardeners carefully timed their own comings and goings not to coincide with the comings and goings of the congregation. In those days, clergy were still quite powerful figures in the community and would not hesitate to admonish those breaking either the Sabbath or Good Friday. In my opinion, working to ensure that your family is well fed is good religion but I remember how careful Dad was about his

Good Friday movements.

An event that stands out occurred at Easter 1922, just before I went into the Boys' School. Arthur Cook, a friend of mine who lived in The Friary, came with me to the allotment and after a while I suppose we became bored - we were only seven. We found two old bill hooks in the shed and proceeded to become cavalry. It was not long before we had to try our swords, as the billhooks had become, on something real and so a row of perfectly harmless Brussells Sprouts were decapitated. Our activities did not go unnoticed, for we caught the eye of Mr. Maple, who was working on his nearby allotment. A shout from him and retribution arrived in the shape of my irate father. He seldom lost his temper, but that day he was cross, rightly so, for fresh greenstuff at that time of the year is priceless.

At the top of the neighbouring allotment was the communal pump, a very simple affair that never ran dry as it was only just above the level of the River Avon, flowing some two hundred yards away. In front of the pump was a tub, in reality half of an old beer barrel. This was kept filled to provide the can of water needed for priming. To work the pump, a can of water was poured into the top, you then pumped the handle like mad and glory be, you had a never ending supply of clear cool water, which I drank, without harm on many occasions. I remember my pride when I grew big enough and strong enough to fetch and carry the two gallon water cans for my father.

11 *The Fair*

When I was small, if I happened to say "It's not fair", as I often did, then my mother's stock reply was, "No, and it won't be till next October." She was of course referring to the Salisbury Annual Pleasure Fair that has been held for three days commencing on the third Monday in October for the last seven hundred years. How we used to look forward to it and how long it seemed to be in coming. Each year on the Sunday — the day before the fair started — the family took the late Sunday afternoon walk down Exeter Street, along St. Nicholas Road, over the fourteenth-century Harnham Bridge to The Swan Inn Field. There we would gaze at the massive steam engines, all ready connected to their huge waggons, to make a quick getaway to The Market Place at dawn on the following day. This was before the building of New Bridge Road and it now seems impossible that the large convoy of vehicles could ever make its way over the narrow bridges leading into the city. Heaven help anyone wanting to travel in the opposite direction on the Monday morning!

To see the fair convoy on the move was a terrific thrill. Those wonderfully powerful steam engines belching out smoke as they literally trembled on their way, the fair men hanging on to all sorts of vantage points as they progressed towards their goal. It never looks half as glamorous today, now that the motive power is diesel. Even when the rides have been erected it seems quite a lot of the fun has vanished. Where we used to see an organ with its automated conductor and maybe a waterfall thrown in for good measure, we now have canned music and disc jockeys aping their favourites from radio or TV and hoping against hope that one day they too may be discovered.

One of my first recollections of the fair was spotting on the Monday evening a toy tool set priced at one shilling on a stall near the Council House (now called The Guildhall). Mum said no, I couldn't have it because she had already spent her money. When we got home, Dad came to the rescue, with the necessary bob (as a shilling was called) and so, on the following day, I became the proud owner of my very own tool set. Proud until I took the tools from the display card and then pride turned to disappointment for I had expected that the tools would be scaled down versions of Dad's but the saw was just a piece of tin stamped out — it wouldn't cut paper and the hammer was similarly made. However I must have played with it for that tool set led to Dad's most embarrassing moment — something which he never ever let me forget.

After work one evening, Dad brought one of his workmates, Harry Acton, home for a cup of tea. Young Arthur was playing with his tool set under the table and during a lull in the conversation was heard to say: "Now, where's my tenon saw — oh course, I lent it to Harry Acton — that bloke never brings anything back." No wonder poor Dad was embarrassed, even though I must have been repeating something that he himself had said. I think it must have been the end of a beautiful friendship.

An incident at the fair in 1920 always caused the family great amusement, although I felt, and still feel, that I acted with great aplomb. On Monday, the first day of the fair, Mum took me down to The Market Place after school and, armed with my fare, I got on to the children's roundabout. This was a simple affair worked by one-man- power, just the turning of a large crank. Mum said, "I'll wait here for you." The ride started and each time that I passed Mum I waved. Then it stopped and I found myself on the side opposite to her. I got off, made my way round but there was no sign of her. As I went one way she must have gone the other. I looked frantically in the milling crowd but instead of panicking, dashed off to Brown Street and so to the premises of Farr's where Dad worked. I ran through the works to find him and he asked what was the matter. It was then that I made my never-to-be-forgotten answer, "Mum's lost, down the fair." Dad went to see Mr. Farr to explain the situation and off we went to find Mum. It was quite easy, for she was standing at the front of the Council House talking to a large policeman and when Dad and I reached them he said, "There you are Mrs. Maidment, I knew he'd turn up like a bad penny!"

I expect young people of today would rate the fair rides of the early 1920's quite tame affairs. Packed into The Market Place would be three roundabouts, three switchbacks, a helter-skelter, chair-o-planes and a cake walk as well as children's roundabouts, stalls and sideshows. The roundabouts had galloping horses, ostriches and other animals beautifully carved in wood and painted by real craftsmen. The other main attraction — switchbacks — had gondolas, each with its carved monster or dragon head and containing seating for about fifteen people. As each ride had five gondolas, it is easy to see why the various fair magnates were wealthy, even in the days when a ride cost 3d. The big names at Salisbury Fair were Anderton and Rowland and Jacob Studtz.

The Cake Walk was supposed to be a most daring ride although if you held the rail whilst progressing around the U-shaped walk as it tossed like a rough sea, it wasn't too bad. Sometimes people lost their footing and brought down others, quickly making a writhing heap on the floor.

Sideshows have varied little over the years. From the time that I was about eight, the Boxing Booth acted as a magnet to me and I spent a considerable time gazing in awe as the boxers paraded on the small stage outside the tent, ready to take on all comers. If a negro was amongst them, the interest was even greater, for at that time Salisbury contained few coloured people. Among the challengers, excellent boxers from the Army who were stationed nearby often took a chance to make an extra pound or two, although if caught, would be for the high jump, as this sort of contest was strictly against regulations. The crowd always wanted the challenger to win, something that did not happen too often, because I remember the timing of the rounds appeared to be fixed to the advantage of the resident boxer.

One year, I was so proud of Dad, who always took me to the Fair on the Tuesday evening, because he won a coconut which I carried home feeling most superior. We stood for some time watching the "Try your strength" machine which was always sited by The Fawcett Statue on Blue Boar Row. One after another, men paid their money, swung the mallet and failed to ring the bell at the top of the standard. Eventually Dad could wait no longer, saying, "I'm going to have a go", and stepped up to pay his tuppence. He was not a big man — only about five feet seven inches tall — but his years as a coachsmith had given him a body that was all muscle with not an ounce of fat. As Longfellow put it in his poem "The Village Blacksmith" — "The Smith a mighty man is he". When an apprentice, after leaving school at thirteen, my father had spent several years as a striker — using a sledgehammer. The technique learned during those years didn't fail him on this occasion, for he stepped forward, swung the bitel in such a way that to my amazement and also that of the onlookers, the disc just sprang up the standard and hit the gong with a resounding clang, whereupon Dad modestly collected his prize of a coconut, handed it to me to carry and we went on our way.

A year or so later his professional technique scored another success. One of the sideshows had a two-inch thick scaffold board into the top of which five-inch nails had been driven to a depth of about half an inch. You were invited to drive the nail through the timber to the other side with one blow from a hammer. A smith uses a hammer very differently to most tradesmen, never holds it at the bottom of the shaft, for the resulting whip means that power is lost so they always clench the tool near the head. One after another, men failed in their attempts to drive

A general view of Salisbury Fair in the 'twenties. The children's roundabouts are on the right.

the nails, usually succeeding in bending them, so I was proud when Dad, using the skill gained over so many years at the anvil, gave his nail an almighty thump sending it through to the other side of the board. The prize, a box of chocolates, looked from the outside, a jolly sight better than they tasted.

Every year on the Wednesday evening, after going up to bed, I used to stand at my window and gaze towards the fair some five hundred yards away, watching the flickering lights and hearing the screams and music, feeling quite sad that the show was over for another year.

12 *"My Gran"*

I only knew one of my grandparents, Grandmother Tapper, as the other three had died long before I was born. I was only about five and a half when she too died after a long illness and one of my earliest recollections is riding in the well, at the foot of her bath-chair when she went out for constitutionals. Gran was born in Rollestone Street, Salisbury in 1837, the year of Queen Victoria's Accession and had much in common with her. For a start, Grandmother too was a small lady, under five feet in height and like the Queen, quite a martinet.

Her life must have been hard for she not only produced ten children, one of whom died in infancy but also gave birth to my mother when in her forty-fifth year. In addition, my Grandfather, for twenty-odd years prior to his death, at the age of seventy two in 1907, suffered from a chest condition which incapacitated him each winter. This was of course in the days prior to National Health Insurance when prolonged illness meant real hardship. My mother used to tell me how Grandmother scrimped and saved during the summer months so that precious golden sovereigns could be put away in a padlocked wooden box to ensure survival during the next winter. Grandfather was a skilled painter and decorator, also able to put his hand to signwriting on occasion. When he was well, he always seemed to be in demand and was proud to have worked on the Salisbury Cathedral restoration in the 1860's, carried out under the direction of the great Victorian architect, Sir Gilbert Scott.

Gran could recall the last outbreak of cholera which hit Salisbury in 1849, it was especially severe in her own parish of Saint Edmund and many people in the city died as a result. A Government commission was set up and a new and clean water supply and sewerage system installed, whilst new cemeteries were laid out just outside the City and burials in the old churchyards forbidden. Another of Gran's memories was witnessing the last public hanging in Salisbury when she was twelve. It took place at the junction of Wilton and Devizes Roads, opposite the County Gaol. Strangely my mother always referred to the area between St. Paul's Road and Gas Lane as "the old Gaol ground", no doubt copying her mother's description for the area was developed for housing in 1870.

When Gran was small, water was obtained at her Rollestone Street home by lifting a trap door in the floor and letting down a container into the stream below. This stream was part of the system installed by Alderman Hussey in the previous century and apparently all sorts of things used to float past. No wonder that the City suffered periodic outbreaks of cholera for Hussey's Hatches were supposed to give a clean and fresh water supply for St. Edmund's and St. Martin's parishes.

After the birth of my mother, when times were hard, Gran became caretaker of St. Mary Magdalene's Church in Gigant Street, a chapel-of-ease to St. Martin's. For this work she received two shillings and sixpence per week, quite a nice sum for the 1880's when farm workers were expected to bring up families on twelve shillings a week. The job had one stipulation — the wooden floor had to be scrubbed completely once a week. Mum told me that she used to help with this before leaving school and recalled just what hard work it was.

When Gran died, she laid in her coffin in the front room prior to the funeral. This was quite a normal thing at that time and neighbours would call to pay their last respects. I remember that between a death and the subsequent funeral the street would be very quiet, pianos were locked, children were not allowed to play anywhere near the house and on the day of interment, all blinds were drawn, whilst as the cortege made its way to the Cemetery people would stop, the men always removing headgear.

Mum lifted me up to see Gran and I recall the peaceful look which she had. Some modern parents would be horrified at this ritual but my mother had the strong belief that as death comes to all, the sooner you learnt about it the better.

I attended the funeral and for a long time afterwards we, as a family, used to take flowers to the grave. It was a long walk, almost a mile each way and as we neared the Lodge Gates, I would look over the Cemetery wall at old tombstones, bearing Christian names which to seemed so strange, Ezekiel, Zachariah, Obidiah and many similar.

There was also a more modern stone having a line of music. This was to the memory of a Cathedral Organist and his bride who were drowned when the motor vessel, *Stella*, hit the Casquet Rocks near Alderney as they went on honeymoon. Mum said that in the opinion of Gran, it was God's judgement — as whilst the bridegroom was almost sixty years of age, his bride was in her early twenties. Mum used add, "and his first wife was hardly cold."

13 Our House

As I wrote earlier, the house where we lived was Church property, having been given to St. Martin's by an eighteenth-century benefactor. The church was an excellent landlord for although the rent for the six-roomed house was modest — seven shillings and a penny per week — this included rates, repairs and decoration. The outside painting was thoroughly carried out every seventh year, the two downstairs rooms — the front room and kitchen, every fourteen. These may seem long periods but the work was so well done that the paintwork was never shabby. Blow lamps were used to strip woodwork, which was then primed, had two undercoats and gloss coated with lead-based paints that are no longer available because of their toxic effect.

The front door had been beautifully oak grained, this is today almost a lost art, although when I was a boy, every painter worth his salt would not only copy woods but also marble. They seemed to work extremely quickly using graining combs, brushes, even feathers to produce finishes in which they took great pride.

The door had a black painted cast-iron knocker, brass numbers and handle that were polished each week, and when I became old enough to be trusted with this job, I felt very grown up. The door step, worn to a curve in the centre was of mid-grey slate rounded on the edge.

The front room was about eleven feet by twelve feet, having a window to the left of the door as you entered. This was quite high, about four feet from the floor with a very wide sill on which rested Mum's aspidistra. She had kept this plant for many years and whenever we had light showers it was popped outside, a treatment that seemed to agree with it. The fireplace, of typical Victorian cast-iron, was in the centre of the left hand wall whilst on the mantlepiece was a marble clock that had been presented to my mother and father when they married in 1904, this had a large china dog on each side. The alcove to the left of the fireplace had a rounded arch at the top with three shelves, chock-a-block with crest china souveniers, so much in fashion during the first quarter of this century. A sofa filled the floor space under the window and this, like the two matching arm chairs, was covered in a dark brown leatherette. The room had one other chair, a red velvet-covered rocker, having massive springs and I well remember how, when sitting on this on one occasion, absent-mindedly put my hand on the bottom leg. I then slightly rocked the chair and my fingers were so badly crushed that, a few weeks later, my blackened finger nails fell out.

On the wall opposite the fireplace hung a framed black and white print, one of those distributed by Pears Soap, round about the 1900's. Called "My Boy", it depicted a mother bidding farewell to a pampered looking son as he went back to prep. school whilst, through the gates, his schoolmates were having a thoroughly good time. I have seen many of these prints which the soap firm issued, they all have one thing in common — sentimentality. Beneath this print was a family heirloom: the centre section of a remarkably old gate leg table. The two leaves and the gates had gone long since, for it possibly dated from the sixteenth century — nevertheless there was a distinct something about it and Mr. Hibberd, the antique dealer often asked my mother if she would consider selling. On the far wall as you entered from the street, to the left, was the piano; the door from the kitchen on the right. All the walls in this room had grained wainscoting to a height of three feet.

The kitchen was an extremely warm and comfortable room of about the same size. The right wall had a cupboard door, with the stair door at the far end; on the space between was a mahogany bookcase which my father had made. This wall was matchboarded to the ceiling, the other three having wainscoting similar to the front room, oak grained, as were the doors. The first step of the stairs was actually in the room, the protruding edge being well rounded to avoid barked shins. In the centre of the opposite wall was a kitchener grate, with a small compact fire only about 12 inches x 10 inches x 10 inches, which not only kept the room beautifully warm, but also provided heat for a quite sizeable oven on the left and a hob large enough to take three saucepans. The four upright bars at the front of the fire made excellent "window" toast. This was toast which was held on a toasting fork and was pressed against the bars so that the bread was scorched, it was then quickly turned ninety degrees so that it finished up with a grid pattern rather like a leaded window.

To the right of the kitchener were two cupboards, the top some five feet high used for airing clothes, the lower containing all the necessary paraphernalia for the stove — blacklead and brushes, metal polish for the shiny parts plus the boot and shoe cleaning materials. In those days no-one ventured out with dirty footwear no matter how poor they were. On the opposite side of the chimney breast was an alcove about four feet wide with three shelves and two deep drawers. This was always termed "the dresser" even though it had no back of its own; china was stored there, cups and jugs hanging from hooks. The top shelf was reserved for one of Mum's wedding presents, a floral decorated bone china tea service, only used on very special occasions, which we all treated with great respect. The window looking out on the yard and garden was magnificent, had twenty panes, each about 12 inches x 10 inches, a beautiful example of workmanship from the eighteenth century, the counterweighted sashes still working perfectly. Under the window was Mum's treadle Singer Sewing Machine, always in use, for not only did she make much of the family's clothes but also dresses and coats for friends, which helped the household purse.

The cover of this machine provided many happy hours for me when tiny. Turned upside down on the floor, it became my boat, my cart, a railway engine — it's amazing what a child can make of a simple object in imagination. Between the window and the panelled door leading to the back kitchen was a section of wall some eighteen inches wide holding a well-designed, ornate oval mirror. I remember that when I had my first Mecanno set, Dad made a simple hoist which was clamped to the table, a pulley was fixed to a hook above the mirror and my Teddy Bear used to go on trips up to the ceiling. In the centre of the room was a deal table with a top that was scrubbed daily, it had a large cutlery drawer and one of the four turned legs was well worn where generations of cats had sharpened their claws. Six windsor chairs surrounded the table. Dad's was a carver and Mum's had shortened legs because, being only 4 feet 10 inches tall, the lower chair was a great help when she was nursing us as babies. The floor, as in all the rooms, was covered in lino and the room was lit by gas — the initial burning of new mantles on this never ceased to be of interest to me.

Going through the door to the back kitchen you had to take three steps down and immediately to the left was the matchboard door to the garden. Next to the door was a small window that nevertheless boasted sixteen panes. To the right of the steps was the gas cooker, a black monster which provided lots of hard work to keep it clean and at the side of this stood my father's wooden tool chest. This was above the site of a filled-in well and was forever damp. The back kitchen was a lean-to, had no ceiling so the slates of the sloping roof were visible and I remember some of the roof timbers were country-cut, still displaying the odd sign of bark.

Next to the tool chest stood another monster: the mangle, with two large wooden rollers. On Monday evenings, at the end of wash-day, which I thought when small was always the worst day of the week, this would be rolled (it was on castors) to the centre of the room. I remember on one such occasion in early 1920, my sister Gladys and I were upstairs in the top back room, looking out of the window, when we heard a terrifying scream. Running downstairs we found that my eldest sister, Gertrude, who had been helping Mum, had caught her fingers in the rollers. She had to bathe them in very hot water every night for months and fortunately the accident left no permanent damage.

On the right at the back of the room was a matchboard door only six feet in height, leading to the scullery which was very confined, being about nine feet by six feet. To the left as you entered was the copper over which hung a galvanised tub used not only on wash days but also for personal baths. These were normally taken in the scullery as the lifting of hot water by bucket from the copper was quite a performance. During extremely cold weather baths were taken in comfort in the front of the kitchen fire after the rest of the family had gone to bed. This meant carrying buckets of near boiling water a distance of eighteen to twenty feet, and emptying meant doing the job all over again in the reverse direction. It was hard work! In front of the door was the only tap in the house, over a plain earthenware sink about five inches in depth from which the water went into a drain underneath. There was no connecting pipe and water often splashed onto my bare knees.

Next to the sink was another matchboard door leading to the lavatory—which had a well-scrubbed wooden seat atop a white glazed, floral decorated bowl bearing an ornate legend which said "Shanks Patent". Back in the scullery to the left of the lavatory door, coal was stored beneath a window; a convenient spot as it had walls on three sides, with loose boards which fitted into slots at either end forming the front. As the coal went down over the winter months, these boards would be taken away to lower the height. At the beginning of Autumn, the Coal Club run by the Church was paid out with interest added at 1/- in the pound and Mum usually bought 15 cwts with this, which lasted almost through the winter. It was not an easy task for the coalman to make deliveries as he had to lump one hundredweight sacks, right through the house, down three steps, duck to miss the top of the door frame to the scullery, then a mighty heave to deposit coal costing one shilling a hundredweight in the exact spot.

The outside yard was about seven feet in width and bordered by the kitchen wall. The scullery to the left and the wall of the neighbour's house on the right made a convenient place for ball games, always provided care was used to keep away from the windows. I remember a painful occasion in 1923 when I was doing my usual thing, kicking a tennis ball into the U-shape formed by the three walls. I would throw the ball hard against the wall, when it bounced back, take a "controlled" kick, all the while imagining myself as one of my St. Martin's heroes. That particular night — it was on a Wednesday evening — instead of keeping the ball low, I returned it with a very uncontrolled kick and bang! It was right through the window, the second pane up on the left hand side. Mum was somewhat cross and suggested that I should go to meet Dad who had gone to his allotment and confess my indiscretion. This I did, and good old Dad was so nice about it, saying he would get a sheet of glass and putty at the week-end.

Saturday came round, Dad arrived home complete with glass and putty, had his dinner, then proceeded to repair the window. He then went to wash his hands whilst I, stupidly, started to play with my beloved ball. Another uncontrolled kick and bang! It happened again, and again it was the same pane. My placid father who was just wiping his hands suddenly became a raging bull! "Go on up to bed", his words being punctuated by hard slaps to my rump. He followed me upstairs, locked the bedroom door from the outside with "That's it, you stay there till tomorrow morning." To be shut away at quarter past two was a salutary lesson for one not yet nine. I wondered how long one could live without food or water? There were no books in the room so all I could do was look out of the window and wait for the quarterly chimes from the Cathedral Clock. It was the longest afternoon that I had known and it was worse when I heard the sound of tea being prepared downstairs for this made me even more hungry. At about six o'clock, I heard Dad going out to a meeting and presently Mum appeared with some food, but insisted I was to stay in my prison till morning. I've often wondered what the odds were against breaking that same pane twice in succession.

The garden was about 14 feet by 50 feet in area and, as Dad was a keen gardener, became a lovely show of flowers each summer. He had built a lean-to greenhouse on the back of the scullery and prided himself on his chrysanthemums and gladioli. Loganberries and raspberries grew on wires at both sides of the garden which had a centre bed with paths around it and beds running next to the fences. At the end of the garden were the two chicken houses, a run for daytime and to the right the sleeping quarters with a tiny window about a foot square. It was a lovely sight to see all the sleeping hens on their perch and exciting to open up the door in the morning to find they had laid eggs for our breakfast in the three nest boxes on the floor. When I was seven, Dad bought me some bantams, a cock and two hens, and these supplied me with my own child-sized eggs. The bantams and chickens always seemed to co-habitate without quarrels, something of a miracle for the bantam cock used to strut around as though he was king of the entire run.

Each spring Dad arranged a treat: exactly three weeks prior to Easter Sunday he would put a dozen fertilised eggs under a broody hen in a portable house and run below the kitchen window, where she was safe from predators. I would arrive home from Morning Service on the big day to find the chicks were fighting their way from the shells. The eggs were always obtained from Ashfords Farm at Milford and never failed to produce chicks. But how did my father calculate the exact timing, or was he just lucky?

Going back inside the house, the two staircases up to the first and second floors were dark as neither had windows, the only light available came from open bedroom doors. All the interior walls were of matchboard and both first floor rooms had sizeable under-stairs cupboards.

My father and mother slept in the room facing the street and when I was small my black cast-iron drop sided cot was placed next to the bed which had a nerer-forgotten picture over it. Called "Suspense", it showed a small girl, saying her prayers before having breakfast in bed, on either side her cat and dog waited in great anticipation. The coloured print was one of the more successful of a series issued by the makers of Pears Soap. I used to gaze at it and wish that I could have a dog just like the one in the picture.

This print, called "Suspense", hung over my parents' bed and from a very early age I wished that I could have a dog like that — have a look at the picture of my Nip on page 110.

I spent the greater part of my first twenty-one years, sleeping in the first floor back, a room somewhat smaller than my mother and father's. It was lit by a large sash window having sixteen panes. The view from this was dominated by the Cathedral only six hundred yards away. I never ceased to be amazed by its proportions and architecture and spent many happy hours during School holidays, sketching this wonderful building. Having always been aware of the Cathedral I've often wondered what impact it has on visitors seeing it for the first time.

My room, like the front, was lit by a gas jet and had a small cast-iron fireplace, though fires were only lit when someone was seriously ill.

The two rooms on the top floor were both beautifully light. From the one at the back was a fine view across the City to Harnham Hill and the Raceplain beyond. These rooms housed two family heirlooms; a tilting-top circular oak table, standing on a pillar with three splayed legs, made by my great-grandfather prior to his wedding, and a patchwork quilt made by Gran Tapper in preparation for her marriage. This had several squares of very heavy, dark grey woollen cloth which Mum told me came from her own great grandmother's cloak, so presumably could well have dated back to the eighteenth century.

14 The Cattle Market

When I was a small boy, almost all cattle and sheep sold in the market were either transported by rail to Milford Goods Station or, if they came from farms within a six-mile or so radius, were driven on the hoof early in the morning. Whichever method was used it meant long traffic holdups as the creatures went through the streets, their already frightened state heightened by a deal of cruelty on the part of many of the drovers. It could not have been easy for these men to deliver flocks and herds safely to their destination and the advent of motor transport must have been a blessing to animals.

Runaways were commonplace, and I remember when a bull, on its way back to Milford Station, thought enough was enough, broke free and terrorised the neighbouring streets for about half-an-hour before recapture. On another occasion, a cow made a mad dash from a herd being driven along Crane Bridge Road, managed to dive onto the slope leading to the old ford by the bridge, took off in the Harnham direction and swam almost a mile before the drovers caught up with her. On Wednesday mornings, the City streets would be strewn with manure, quickly gathered by keen gardeners armed with buckets and shovels.

The market had many well-known characters and two spring immediately to mind. Mr. John Jeffery, the auctioneer, looked himself every inch a farmer and had a wonderfully fruity voice that carried a long way. He used to be chauffeur-driven to market and one evening, when returning via Lower Road, Bemerton, on the way back to his home at Donhead, saw a small child in the water, being swept downstream by the fast-flowing River Nadder. Mr. Jeffery ordered his man to stop, rescued the child and went on his way.(It is interesting to note that the Jeffery family have been in Donhead for centuries as The Visitation of Wilts 1565 records that the first wife of Alderman Thomas Pople of Salisbury, was "Katherine, daughter to John Jeffery of Doned Marie,

Dorset".)

Another very well-known character was Mr. George Penny, the horse dealer from Petersfinger. Each Market Day, from lunchtime on, his trap, with a very patient pony in the shafts, could been seen waiting outside The Cathedral Hotel in Milford Street. During the afternoon, Mr. Penny would somewhat unsteadily make his way to the trap, get in, flop down and lightly pick up the reins; the pony knowing what had to be done would start off, quickly breaking into a spanking trot as he made his way along Milford Street. Meanwhile, his master, all eighteen or so stone of him would loll back on one of the side seats, making no effort to drive. I can see that pony now, lifting its feet in a lovely trot, take the sharp rise at Milford Hill, perform a right turn into Rampart Road, then a left turn into Southampton (now Tollgate) Road, past the Milford Railway Goods Station to safely deliver Mr. Penny to his home. Such a performance would be impossible in today's heavy traffic, an accident surely the outcome.

Horses to be sold in the market were always tethered to the iron railings along Ox Row, sheep being penned nearby, with cattle towards Blue Boar Row. In the centre would be several lines of trestle tables carrying cages for chicken, ducks and geese with a few tame rabbits. The dead stock was usually sold in one or other of the privately owned auction marts.

The thought of caged chicken reminds me of the occasion — I was about seven at the time — when my father lost his rather large, pompous cockbird who dominated his twelve wives.

When Dad fed them on the Sunday evening, he was still in the run as usual, but when my father opened up on Monday morning, the bird was missing. It was impossible for him to have escaped on his own for the door was secured by a wedge, pushed through a hasp to hold the hinged staple in place. Obviously a thief had been about, but Dad had no time to investigate before setting off for work.

Fortunately the incident took place during the school holidays, otherwise I would not have been in the garden later in the morning, when a cock started crowing. The sound came from over the garden wall and I knew that no-one in that part of Gigant Street kept chicken. Without telling anyone, I climbed to the top of the brick wall, looked over, it had about a nine foot drop on the other side and there in a Tate Sugar Box with a slatted front was a caged cockbird. I was sure that it was my father's.

It seemed an eternity before Dad arrived home at one o'clock and he hardly had time to get indoors before I blurted out just what I had discovered. Off went Dad to the bottom of the garden, looked over the wall and there was C....... W........, the eldest son of the house, looked upon as a ne'er-do-well, gazing at his prize. Dad wasted no words and said that it was his bird in the box whereupon C....... tried to brazen out the situation by saying he had found the cockbird in the garden and was taking it to the market in the morning.

"Can I help it if it flew over the wall?"

At this, Dad lost his temper — either the bird was brought round straight away or he was calling the police. The bird was returned by a badly shaken youth, who gave no more trouble and, for a few hours, I was Dad's blue-eyed boy.

At the end of Market Day, the animals had to be driven away. A few made a short journey, for most privately owned butchers, there were still over twenty of them in the city, operated their own slaughter-houses. For the remainder it was back to Milford Station where they were probably penned overnight on the extremely wide platforms, before dispatch the next day in newly lime-washed trucks. All trucks had to be well-hosed and limewashed between each and every journey. The job was carried out by piece workers who did rather well financially from carrying out what was a pretty filthy job.

Meanwhile, throughout the day, The Market House was a hive of activity, with the selling of corn and other farming commodities. The centre section was surrounded by some forty or fifty high desks staffed by representatives of member traders. On the left hand side, goods trains ran right into the building — this short railway, operated by The Salisbury Railway and Market House Company, had the shortest operating track in Britain and connected with The London and South Western Railway near the main-line station. Outside in The Cheese Market at the corner of Castle Street and Blue Boar Row, traders who paid no tolls were always to be found on the same spot each Market Day. For instance, should a farmer require some fencing, he knew that Mr. Green would be on the edge of the pavement at the right hand corner of The Market House — a position that Green's had occupied over generations. So it was with many others, selling implements, rope and all the other necessities needed by the farming community. At the end of the day the pavements in this area would be covered with corn-samples discarded after a deal had been struck — the farmer would plunge his hand into his pocket, produce a sample which would be carefully examined by the dealer and then onto the ground went the handful to be gratefully devoured in due course by the rapidly growing pigeon population.

Few cheapjacks went to the Tuesday market, but there were numerous stalls selling vegetables, fish, clothing and many other items. Nearly all stallholders were local, either from the city or surrounding countryside. In the summer, strawberry sellers usually took up position around the Crimean Cannon at the side of The Council House and they had to dispose of all their perishable wares before returning home. The resulting knock-down sale at the end of the day was eagerly awaited by many people, who were able to buy a basket for 6d.

The Market Place, after the removal of the animals, would be covered in straw and slurry. Horse-drawn Corporation open-sided dust carts and perhaps a dozen men were brought into action and, after disposal of the worst of the refuse, the surface was well hosed. During this operation, the market was not a place for the general public. On one occasion a friend of mine, resplendent in new sports jacket and flannels, rather unwisely walked across the diagonal market path. He passed within six feet of a cart, on the opposite side to the working men, received a shovel full of slurry on the shoulders and chest, which one of those individuals, either by accident or design, had thrown right over the vehicle. Although the City Council paid the bill for dry cleaning he never forgot the smell or the indignity of walking through the City streets on a summer evening drenched in manure.

Doubtless, Salisbury traders benefitted from the weekly market despite the disruption to normal traffic. Life seventy years ago was at a slower pace and people were able to cope more easily with upset routines. The pubs especially were somewhat dependent on the influx of people from the countryside and after all, for the rest of the population, the kerfuffle was only one day each week.

15 *"Ee Bah Goom"*

During August 1920, my two maiden aunts, Rachel and Gertrude, my mother's sisters, took me to Preston in Lancashire on a week's visit to a fourth sister, Aunt Fan. Her husband, Uncle George, and their two daughters, Maggie and Marie, were like her, extremely short — not one of them would have reached the five foot mark.

We did not make a direct trip for we took the train to London, then I made my first underground journey to Finsbury Park, the most northerly point on the tube at that time. From there, we took an open top bus to Tottenham where my Uncle Arthur lived with his wife, Aunt Annie. This was the first time I had been to the house and it seemed enormous. Not only did the street door open on to a wide passage, but there were three large rooms downstairs, plus a scullery, the front room having a bay window. Upstairs were four bedrooms and a bathroom, with hot water being supplied via a gas geyser. The house seemed quite grand but we only stayed one night as the following afternoon we entrained for Preston, a journey that took so long, I wondered if we would ever arrive. On the way, I remember Aunt Rachel telling me that a station was Rugby, which meant that we were then right in the centre of England, whilst a bit later on, I was told to look out to see the Welsh mountains. Arriving at Preston, I had another first, riding in a motor taxi to St. Paul's Road, our destination.

One day, we paid a visit to Blackpool, where my cousins took me, much against my wishes, on a water chute. We had to climb what seemed a never-ending staircase to a high platform where we took our seats in a punt at the top of a slide having water rushing down it. As soon as we got there, I started yelling for I was really scared, thought I should drown, but the grown-ups just laughed and off we slid, down the steep slope to hit the water with a mighty splash, then gently floated to the other side of the pool to disembark. This episode put me off water for years, the platform had seemed almost as high as the Blackpool Tower which we had just visited.

On another day we went to St. Anne's where I played on the sands that were not a patch on those of the South Coast. The adults, in the way that grown-ups have, forgot that my ears were listening and talked with bated breath of the murder that had taken place on those very sands earlier that year. A man had shot a woman, buried her body in the sands, had been caught and hung for his crime. I listened to this tale of woe and as I dug with my tiny spade, wondered what I might find, an arm or perhaps a leg, but the only discoveries that I made were small pieces of coal washed up on the beach.

Both my cousins were operators in a cotton mill where Uncle George was a maintenance fitter, a job which had left its mark for he was minus a finger on each hand. One day we went for a tour around the mill and the lasting memory that I have is the terrible clattering of the looms and the speed at which the never idle operators worked to ensure that their piece of material was faultless. I also remember how the knocker-up went around the streets banging at bedroom windows with a long stick to wake the occupants in time to get to work. He was followed shortly afterwards by the sound of wooden clogs on cobble stones as people hurried to the mill before the hooter started.

The Lancashire dialect seemed like a foreign language to me although the people were kind. Uncle George showed me his collection of Preston North End memorabilia, dating from the period 1888 to 1902, when as a young man he had been a staunch supporter of "The Invincibles" who won both The Football Association Cup and Division I of The Football League in the same season. Since then I have always followed the fortunes of Preston and am saddened to see them languishing in the lower divisions.

It was during my visit that I made my acquaintance with Woolworths and thought it a marvellous store with goods that were priced at either 3d or 6d; the firm did not arrive in Salisbury until 1927.

Some forty-five years after my visit to Preston I was talking to a business acquaintance who, although having been based in Southampton for many years, had never lost his Lancashire accent. I asked him from which part of that county he came and when he said Preston, I told him of my own connections and was amazed to find that his parents had kept the shop in St. Paul's Road where I had gone to buy sweets in

I REMEMBER, I REMEMBER

1920. It really is a small old world.

I make no apology for the title of this chapter because it was an expression which my cousins used very frequently.

16 *The Carnival Spirit*

A highlight for me, in 1921, was the Saint Martin's Carnival, held during the summer to aid Church Funds. For a purely parochial event, it must have been quite an occasion because I believe that it ran from Wednesday, through to the following Saturday. As is usual with a carnival, it started with a Fancy Dress Procession around the parish, which finished at the Shady Bower Field, and a great deal of thought went into the entries. The winners in the Adult Section were my Aunt Gertrude and her friend, Miss Alice Pearce, who were ideally suited for their chosen parts of Darby and Joan. Whilst my aunt was a small, slightly built, lovable shy lady, her friend was large, buxom and to me somewhat frightening, although she made a wonderful Darby. As a pair they really were an excellent entry and looking back, I am somewhat amazed that my aunt ever plucked up the courage to parade around the streets. I still remember the long black gloves that she wore.

I became a Market Gardener and my parents and sisters spent a lot of time not only on my costume but also in the decoration of my wheelbarrow. This had been made by Dad some time previously, it was a beautifully constructed scaled-down version of the wooden barrows in use at that time. I often took it with me when going to the allotment and felt very grown up on the return journey if my father had put a few vegetables in it.

For the carnival the barrow was filled with vegetables and two wire half hoops straddled it from front to back and side to side, these were beautifully decorated with flowers by my sisters and the wheelbarrow really did look effective. As for me, I wore a white countryman's smock that Mum had made, had a red handkerchief tied around my neck and a floppy grey felt hat with wide brim was stuck on my head.

I won second prize, being beaten by a boy named Bryant, who the following month emigrated with his family to South Africa. He had gone in a very simple costume as "The Kid". The film of that title, a Charlie Chaplin classic, had recently been shown in Salisbury, "the Kid" being played by Jackie Coogan. My prize was a voucher for half-a-crown which had to be spent on one of the Carnival's stalls. Whilst I was wondering just what I might buy with it, the problem was solved when Mum bought me a grey shirt. Rather unreasonably, I felt somewhat cheated for I had been the one to traipse around the town, forgetting all the preliminary work that others had done!

During the carnival, an open air Pierrot Show was in operation in front of the Shady Bower Pavilion and there were numerous side shows around the field. My eldest sister had a black cauldron suspended from an old iron cooking tripod, this was filled with sawdust and packed with small gifts which made for an attractive lucky dip at tuppence a time.

One of the side shows which brought unfortunate consequences for me, was "Breaking up the Happy Home". Old crockery was displayed on a series of shelves and for 2d you got three wooden balls and could smash the crockery to your heart's content. I wanted to have a go but being not yet seven was refused, however the sideshow gave me an idea. The following morning I got Dad's step-ladder out, put some of his flowerpots from the greenhouse on the steps and was having a lovely time with my own version of "Breaking up the Happy Home" when the sound of pots smashing brought my carnival to an end. I thought that a smacked bottom and being sent to bed very early that evening was hardly just reward for aping my elders.

Another amusing memory of the Carnival is of The Comic Football Match played with a Rugby ball. One of the leading lights among the event's organisers was Mr. Roland Gordon, the son of the Assistant Priest. He was a civil servant, on leave from India where he was a stipendiary magistrate. An austere looking man who seldom smiled, he entered into the spirit of the occasion for not only was he a Pierrot but also Captain of one of the football teams. Mr. Harry Payne captained the other side and, instead of a normal kick-off, the two gentlemen bullied off in hockey fashion, Mr. Gordon with a wooden-shafted golf club, his opponent with a cricket bat. The referee blew a toy trumpet and Harry Payne gave the golf club a mighty hit with his bat, breaking the shaft in two. Mr. Gordon stumped off the field, holding the two pieces of broken club and giving vent to language ill-befitting the lay-reader son of a clergyman — "my best bloody driver, my best bloody driver." The onlookers at first thought this accident was part of the show and were creased with laughter, making the poor man even more irate.

Mr. Gordon came back to Salisbury upon retirement, was Councillor for St. Martin's Ward, then Mayor of the City and did a grand job in cataloguing the City's Archives.

17 *"Pantos" and "Flicks"*

In the 'twenties, Salisbury possessed three places of entertainment, The Palace Theatre in Endless Street at The Chipper Lane Corner, The Picture House in Fisherton Street and The New Theatre in Castle Street. The Palace had been built in 1889 as The County Hall and was a magnificent example of the art of bricklaying — it held 1,100 people. Until the closure in 1931, not only revues and plays were staged, but also star films were shown. Many well known artistes played The Palace including Gracie Fields. It was also used for local productions by The Dramatic and Operatic Societies and I remember for a number of years the Bishop Wordsworth School Prizegiving was held there.

The Picture House in Fisherton Street had been built in 1869 as a Primitive Methodist Chapel but, after closure in 1915 when a replacement was built in Dews Road, became a cinema. A not unpleasant façade was added which brought the front out to the street. I remember this had "The Picture House" in relief Roman lettering just below the parapet and as a boy I was puzzled by the two V's in place of the U's. Later on I realised that Architects were going through a Classical phase and as the Romans had no U in their alphabet V was substituted, and I've wondered since how a hard headed business man like Albany Ward was taken for a ride by his architect.

The New Theatre in Castle Street was built very hurriedly in 1915 to provide entertainment for the troops. It was a real utility cinema — one storey, no balcony and no frills, excepting a canopy which straddled the pavement. The roof girders were open for all to see.

In the 'twenties, all three were owned by cinema magnate, Mr. Albany Ward, who had seized the opportunity offered by the presence of so many troops stationed in South Wiltshire during the war to provide entertainment for them. Many villages to the west of Salisbury had either their own cinemas or one of Albany Ward's Palaces of

Variety. In addition, he obtained a virtual monopoly on advertising sites and also started The Salisbury Press Limited in Wilton Road to provide the ever increasing publicity needs for his cinema and theatre chain.

My earliest visit to The Palace was to see a pantomime, something for which it had a reputation. We always went on Boxing Day and every year the show seemed to include not only Shetland Ponies but also waterfalls. To a child, at least in my day, pantomimes were so real — a trip into another world, fairy tales coming to life. The finale was always a wonderful climax, with the central staircase — the cast coming from left and right, bouncing down the steps to take up position on stage and then the best moment of all when the principal boy and girl arrived, coming down the stairs hand-in-hand to live happily ever after.

I remember too, that the audience used to participate in singing a song, the words being on a large sheet unrolled from the roof of the

This photograph of the Palace Theatre in Endless Strreet, clearly shows the art of Victorian bricklayers. The Deputy Town Clerk, Mr Walter Carey, is standing in the doorway of the Municipal Offices to the left.

stage. Occasionally these songs were somewhat risque although it was many years before I became aware of any double meaning. One of them ran —

January, February, March, April and May
Jack and Jill went up the hill,
Not for water, we know but still,
June July and August
They marry and what they do,
September, October, November, December
Is nothing to do with you.

They were wonderful shows and The Palace always seemed to be packed for them.

Each year, during the Christmas Holidays, all children between the ages of seven to fourteen and attending the City's Elementary schools were invited by Mr. Albany Ward to a free Film Matinee at The Palace. The first that I went to in 1922 was quite a treat. The film, silent of course, was a New York Detective Drama and the murder weapon, a spanner was hidden behind a radiator. After the show, as we left, we each received a large orange and a shiny new penny. It may seem ungrateful, but that orange was as sour as anything I have ever tasted — it brought tears to the eyes. The next year the matinee was repeated — even the same film was shown — the murder weapon was still behind the same radiator, something which most of the audience remembered and shouted the fact loudly to the detective. I expect Mr. Ward thought the behaviour unforgiveable but it's a job to spoof children.

The Palace's one and only commissionaire was a large pompous gentleman named B...... B...... who loved the authority the position gave him. This eventually went to his head, for he later offered himself as a candidate for the City Council. Choosing his moment well, he was returned unopposed at a By-election and proved to be a pretty useless member. When I was out with my father just after Clr. B's election, we met him and Dad asked how the Council was going. He replied that he had been put on the General Purposes and also The Finance Committee. Dad said,

"What do you know about Finance, then?"

"Oh that's easy. I just watch my good friend, Alderman Bracher, and what he votes for, I put my hand up too."

However, when the Council processed on Civic occasions, he really came into his own. His huge bulk, arrayed in scarlet robe and surmounted by a black tricorn hat, really looked most impressive.

The Picture House in Fisherton Street continued as a Cinema until 1937, was empty until becoming a Recruiting Office in 1939, then became The Garrison Theatre in 1943, The Arts Theatre in 1947 and finally The Playhouse before the building of the present theatre. It was my favourite cinema as a boy and the first talkie was shown there in 1930. Admission to the front stalls cost 4d,children cost 2½d and were admitted via a separate entrance in Chapel Place. The pay-box, in a small vestibule, was only occupied prior to the start of the show and the street door had to be left open as a fire exit. The men's toilet was leading off the vestibule near the Pay Box and it was amazing that as soon as the cashier made her way back through the cinema, men would feel a sudden urge to visit the toilet, though in reality they used to push open the street door to let in friends. This dodge must have cost Mr. Ward a lot of money over the years.

The Commissionaire, Mr. Snook, was a nice harmless old gentleman. If he wished to cross from one side of the cinema to the other he had to walk in front of the Orchestra Pit in a crouching position and should the poor old chap not crouch low enough his shadow would appear on the screen bringing, to his great embarrassment, whistles and catcalls from the audience.

The one drawback at The Picture House was the closeness of the seating which meant that the knees of the average size person were thrust into the back of the person in front. The only answer was to sit sideways and hope that your neighbour sat in the same direction.

The New Theatre had a short life of about sixteen years — closing in the Spring of 1932. It never possessed atmosphere and mostly showed second-rate films. The Children's Matinees on Saturdays were extremely popular —the cost was 2½d for all seats and there was always a serial: the forerunners of today's TV soaps. I very seldom went unless it was too wet for football or cricket. On one occasion just before the start of the show I dropped my bomb on the floor and the resulting bang was notwithstanding the usual hubbub, heard by the Commissionaire. A bomb comprised two pieces of lead, held together by string and caps were inserted between the lead, so that when dropped it did cause a fair old bang. The commissionaire came running,

"Who did that?"

My friends around me, loyal to the core, replied in unison,

"He did."

"Right, outside you," and a very embarrassed small boy crept out, past rows of children now wearing superior looks. I waited under the canopy by the paybox — heard the cheer when the film started, waited a few more minutes and was just about to go home when the Manager came out —

"What are you waiting for, son?"

"Been sent out, sir"

"What for?"

When I told him he said,

"If I let you back in, you won't do it again, will you?"

"No Sir, course not Sir."

"Right then — I think I'll keep your bomb until after the show."

"Yes sir, thank you, sir," and a very relieved boy took his place among his so-called friends. It taught me a sharp lesson and, needless to say, I never mentioned a word about it at home for my mother and father would have been really cross and I would have had a lecture for letting the family down.

18 *Shades of W.G.*

During the summer holidays of 1922, I became hooked on cricket, a love that has lasted throughout my life. We had a young lady staying with us for a week or two; she worked with my aunt at Bromley in Kent. One morning she took me to do some shopping. As we passed the window of Curry's in Butcher Row I spotted a cricket set and shekindly bought it for me. It consisted of a bat, four stumps and a rubber ball, the cost all complete on a display card, one shilling and sixpence.

As soon as we got back home I went off to gather a few friends and we made our way to The Greencroft — hardly an ideal spot for cricket, the grass being too long. In fact, the only time it became short was after horses had been tethered there for a treat at week-ends, then we had circles which were fit to play on. The set lasted some time and for a short period, as owner, the first innings was mine. After a while my friends got fed up with bowling and fielding so a limit was placed on a batsman's innings, if you were still not out after three overs you had to retire. The three overs were usually bowled by different bowlers so that everyone had a fair crack of the whip.

It was not long before the rubber ball was replaced by one made of cork, costing sixpence from Wilton's Sports Shop at the corner of Queen Street and The Canal. They were very hard with no give and, as the bat was made from one piece of wood, every time you hit the ball your hands received quite a jar. However it wasn't manly to play the game with a soft rubber ball — that was cissie in the eyes of eight-year-olds. Those games of elementary cricket were wonderful: you learnt to field, to catch, and never to make a fuss about getting hurt, which you often did, for we had no pads or batting gloves as protection. Most of all you acquired an appetite for the game.

I had already started to watch the Saint Martin's Cricket Team who played at Shady Bower (a lovely name) every other Saturday. The field was bounded on one side by Shady Bower Road from which it was divided by an avenue of mature beech trees. To the west was a line of tall elms, part of the Forbes estate, whilst to the south it bordered Milford Goods Station and on the fourth side to the east ran the main railway line from Salisbury to Southampton. Those batsmen hitting sixes were never popular if the ball had to be retrieved from amongst the goods wagons on the lines.

The field, church property, had only primitive facilities, although in this respect it was no worse than most others in the Salisbury and District Cricket League, with the exception of grounds belonging to Army or Air Force units. The only section actually mown was the pitch on which a twelve-inch hand-propelled mower was used. The rest of the grass was kept reasonably short by cart horses that were turned out to graze each evening, although they did cause a hazard by leaving droppings all over the place. The pavilion over in the corner of the ground was brick built and had two wooden flaps that were lifted up to horizontal position, held in place by metal rods to provide shelter for the trestle tables used by the scorers.

I often think when I pass our local playing field, see the beautifully shorn ground with sight-screens and the village teams playing in immaculate whites, just how times have changed in seventy years. In 1922, St. Martin's, one of the leading local sides, turned out in varied attire, a few in white flannels, some in grey, one even in brown tweed for there was little money left to buy things not used every day. At least the umpires wore correct attire of long white coats. Mr. Tom Clarke, who always carried out the job for St. Martin's, was a tall dignified-looking man with white hair. He was a fine shoemaker and for many years Secretary of The Salisbury and District Football League.

The Saints' opening pair at that time was composed of Mr. Ernie Carpenter and Eno Burton. Ernie Carpenter was a slightly built, bespectacled man, a stonewaller most difficult to dislodge. Apart from being a left-hander, his attire of brown tweed trousers and brown trilby hat must have helped to put the bowlers off. Eno Burton, another left-hander, was stocky, powerfully built and hit the ball well — when he connected, but his drawback was that he had the idea that he should hit every delivery to the boundary. I still remember his batting gloves for the thumb pad was separate from the padded fingers to which it was attached by wide elastic that went thrice round the hand before fitting on the thumb. Mr. Windust, our deputy headmaster, usually went in first wicket down. "Windy" was a batsman in more classic style and was good for runs until, as so often happened, he lost his wicket, due to the unpredictable bounce of the pitch. Then followed Aubrey Searle, a good all-rounder and possibly the best slow bowler in the local league. Next came George, his brother, who would thrash about and, should he connect, his powerful physique ensured that the ball went a long, long way. The middle order consisted of three of Dad's boyhood friends — Ernie Rattue, Ted Warren and E.P. or Pearly Adlam. Mr. Rattue was a staid man, whom Shakespeare might have described as "with full round belly." He too wore spectacles and though he never made big scores, stayed around for a long time.

Ted Warren had been an opener for several years before the war. He too had excellent but few scoring strokes but Pearly Adlam was very different, getting his runs by judicious prods and cuts that would have brought him greater reward if the outfield of long grass had not put a brake on his efforts. Teddy Bruton, a postman, never shone with the bat but was a good wicketkeeper, well above league average. During late July and August the team was fortunate enough to have the services of another schoolmaster, Mr. Prince, the son of the Saint Ann's Street postmaster.

As a batsman he was in a different class to the rest, he had a wonderful eye and sense of timing. His one fault was that he never dressed to suit the occasion for he put the rest of the team to shame when he turned out in white flannels, white cricket boots, multi-coloured college blazer and cap, so different to poor Mr. Carpenter's brown suit and trilby! When Prince went in, an air of anticipation could be felt among the spectators and they were seldom disappointed for the game took on a new tempo and small boys putting up the score on the board suddenly had to put a jerk in their work.

On the somewhat under-par pitches of the 'twenties a team score of one hundred or above was a rare event and it should be remembered that to score a boundary the ball's first bounce would need to be within fifteen feet or so of the fence to beat the long grass.

Mr. Lapham, the St. Martin's scorer was a very short man, only about four feet seven inches in height. He would bustle to his table just outside the pavilion and sheltered by the raised flaps, take the score book from its waterproof cover, open it, take four beautifully sharpened pencils from his top pocket, place one on each side of the book, one behind each ear and he was ready for the fray. His knowledge of the rules was first-class and I recall an occasion, when the Saints were playing The City Police, when the Police umpire gave Mr. Ernie Rattue out. On his return to the pavilion, still protesting, Mr. Rattue asked Mr. Lapham for a ruling and armed with the rule book both returned to the crease where the decision was reversed. It didn't make an awful lot of difference for Ernie only received two more balls, the first being dispatched to the boundary for four, the next bowling him, neck and crop, but at least he was happy, having proved his point.

In 1924, someone gave me a small score book which I took along to matches, for it opened up another facet of the game for me. It was quite a fascinating pastime and after the captain of the side taking first innings had written the team's batting order in the official score book, I would go along to Mr. Lapham and shyly ask if I could copy the names. He was most kind and, finding that I was really keen, allowed me to sit at his side to learn how to do the job properly. I owed him a great deal.

Prior to that time, I had just been one of the army of small boys scrabbling to put up the numbers on the score board. Now I was promoted and had the temerity to shout to my mates, "Ten up", "Twenty up" and, from time to time, pop out to make sure the correct score was being shown.

St. Martin's, should they win the toss, always batted first so that after tea their opponents would have to face the really fast bowling of Windy, coming out of the sun with a background of tall elms. Years later in my own playing days, I came to realise just how difficult this was for it was only too easy to lose sight of the ball.

At Winterslow, a different ploy was followed, for if they won the toss, they asked their opponents to bat. At the tea interval, Mr. Horner's celebrated Wiltshire Dough Cake was served hot and after two slices apiece the visitors' fielding suffered. Running after eating hot Dough Cake is a dangerous occupation.

The Saint Martin's teas were served by Mr. Walter Shipsey who used to walk from his bakery in St. Ann's Street to Shady Bower, a distance of half-a-mile, carrying two large wicker baskets, one on each arm. In one, the food, bread and butter ready prepared, slices of fruit cake and pots of jam. The other basket contained cutlery and crockery.

St. Martin's Men's Club in Milford Hill. The site is now covered by the Ring Road.

He would arrive at about 3.30 pm after the match had been in progress for an hour, proceed to erect trestle tables in the pavilion and get the tea urn on the go. From one of his baskets he produced beautifully white tablecloths to cover the decrepit table tops. A tea cost only ninepence, so that the total cash taken could not have been much over a pound — a lot of work for little.

When I was about nine years of age, a friend, Frank Brown, asked if I would help him carry the cricket bag. This meant collecting it from the club in Milford Hill and taking it to Shady Bower, a distance of half-a-mile. That bag containing all the gear was mighty heavy, we took a handle apiece and seemed to change hands almost every fifty yards. It was a long way for two small boys and after the match we had to lug it all the way back again. Our reward was a cup of tea and a slice of fruit cake apiece and the feeling that we were almost part of the team.

Another of Dad's old friends was Mr. Fred Hart, the Secretary of the Salisbury and District Cricket League. Each Saturday he would walk to every game played within the City boundaries, then write the reports for inclusion in the next edition of *The Salisbury Times*, where he worked for many years as a proof reader. He walked very upright, had a trim moustache and his whole bearing was military. Other city clubs in the league included St. Marks, Harnham, The Free Churches (who played at Britford Lane) and the Police. Teams from the district that I remember were Experimental Station at Porton, Cholderton, Royal Air Force, Old Sarum, Winterslow, Downton, Norman Court (the Washington Singer Estate) and Mottisfont. The latter possessed a demon bowler; it was a pity that he could not have been filmed in slow motion, for I felt there was the semblance of a throw in his very low, fast action. Mr. Scott, the Headmaster of Saint Mark's School was another excellent all rounder whilst Mr. Robey of Harnham was always good for a hard hitting innings. I think he struck the ball almost as powerfully as Botham but, not having the same wonderful eye, his innings were never of long duration. Other names that come to mind are E.M. Gollin of Free Churches, a fast bowler, and Captain Eckersley of Experimental Station, Porton, who played some fine innings in classic style.

As boys, we spent every available minute during evenings, Saturday mornings and holidays at Shady Bower. Generally a knock-about game of cricket was in progress, with equipment of the hand-me-down variety, which had seen better days. The wicket, more often than not, was a stick with a coat thrown over to give it width. As bats, even the almost worn-out sort were always in short supply, most games were single wicket, with both sides fielding, which made runs difficult to get. The team captains were appointed because they were either older or bigger than the rest, the bat would be tossed in the air by one of them, the other called "flats" or "rounds". If successful, he then had first choice of available players, then the other captain took his pick, this was done in turn until everyone was allocated, whereupon the bat was again tossed, this time for the right to first innings. Sometimes there could be as many as fifteen a side, then when a newcomer arrived with, "Any chance of a game?", he had to wait until someone else turned up, when the selection into the teams followed. It was almost unknown for anyone to be refused. Arguments did occur as to whether a batsman was out, but generally the games were good-humoured and were played with a lot of effort going into them.

On hot days we got very thirsty but fortunately there was always a solution to the problem. At the end of the field were two railway cottages and in one lived Mr. Ottaway, a retired signalman and very patient. We would all troop down to the wire fence and shout, "Mr. Ottaway, Mr. Ottaway", and this benevolent gentleman would appear, sucking away on an old pipe and carrying a large floral jug filled with lovely cold water which was passed around from boy to boy. Woe betide anyone who was greedy. If there were many of us, Mr. Ottaway refilled the jug until all had a drink. Then he always said "Anyone want any more" and the ritual was repeated. It was not very hygienic, but that water tasted far better than any champagne.

Sometimes the games continued until it was too dark to see the ball. As a result of the hours spent, you got your eye in to all sorts of bowling. It was wonderful practice, cricket played in the true spirit, no umpires to control the game, worn out equipment, but we got tremendous pleasure from it.

In the mid-'twenties an Annual Cricket Match was played between St. Martin's and Bowerchalke Schools, each school playing at home in alternate years. Thanks to the help and encouragement given to me by Mr. Lapham, from 1925 I became the scorer for these matches and have vivid memories of the upheaval preceeding the 1926 fixture at Shady Bower. For the school house matches, involving teams other than my own, I was scorer and also had to prepare the lists of leading batsmen and bowlers for the notice board.

Early in the week before the Bowerchalke match the team list went up with a resulting undercurrent of disagreement. "Bluett" Smith from The Friary had been omitted even though he had been in the team the previous year. Things came to a head during dinner break on Friday when "Bomber" Bailey and "Ginger" Horne, two of our best batsmen, went to Mr. Edwards, who was in charge of cricket, to say they would not play unless their friend "Bluett" Smith was included in the team.

As soon as we reached the classroom in the afternoon "Sammy" Edwards told the assembled classes, six and seven, of the ultimatum that he had been given. He then called on me to fetch the score book which was kept in the Headmaster's room. When I had done this, he said,

"You won't find Smith's name on the list of leading scorers, so perhaps Maidment you can tell us just how many runs he has made?"

I remember the grand total for four innings was three — 2, 1, 0, 0. As I was reading, hissed threats were coming from the Friary trio in Standard Seven.

"We'll get you after school Maidment."

How I was to blame heaven alone knows.

Mr. Edwards then dealt with the problem in a way that I remembered through my business life when faced with similar situations. With no further ado he announced that as Bailey and Horne did not wish to play, their places would be taken by Tibbenham and Tiller. There was no further argument for the Friary trio were dumbfounded and I did not get beaten up after school.

Next day the game was played, Smith, Bailey and Horne were conspicuous by their absence and St. Martin's scored a resounding victory, thanks in no small part to a good innings by Gordon Tibbenham, one of the substitutes.

19 *"Romsey in the Mud"**

Although Romsey is only some fifteen miles from Salisbury, a trip to see my Aunt Rose was quite an occasion. We had the long walk to the London and South Western Railway Station (Salisbury still had a Great Western Station) and then a leisurely ride via Dean and Dunbridge, it was a great experience! Usually I accompanied my Aunt Gertrude on these fairly regular visits and although only afternoon and early evening outings, they seemed to go on for ever.

I made the most of the train ride which never bored me. As soon as we were through the Salisbury tunnel I was on the look out for well known places now seen from a different viewpoint. The Salisbury School Playing Field, Wain-a-Long Road, the Brooks cottage in Laverstock Road, Milford Goods Station and then the footpath across the meadows to Milford Bridge, a favourite Sunday walk.

After this we entered foreign territory, soon came to Alderbury Junction, then the sighting of The Pepperbox, sitting on the hilltop about one and a half miles away. Dean Station always seemed a hive of industry, mainly I suppose because most goods as well as people travelled by train. On now through quite picturesque country to Dunbridge, a most exciting stop for it had an overhead railway system that carried sand and gravel in skips from pits at the top of a ridge about five hundred yards away, over the railway to works on the other side of the station. The total length of this system, carried on pylons some fifty to sixty feet high, was over half a mile and I never tired of watching the slowly moving skips, the full ones on one cable, the empties climbing up again to the ridge on another.

There was a wooded area just outside Dunbridge — once through

* *"Romsey in the Mud" was an expression often heard in the 'twenties, hence the title of the chapter.*

The start of many outings — the Southern Railway Station c. 1926.

this, the line followed the River Test to Romsey, where the station always appeared shabby compared with Salisbury. The population of this ancient borough was at that time only about five thousand and trade had suffered because of its proximity to its thrusting neighbour, Southampton.

On alighting from the train we had to go downstairs, cross under the line through a damp, whitewashed subway to the ticket office where quite often the tickets were taken by Mr. Crabb, who had been at school in Salisbury with my mother's family. His sister was the mother of my great friend Alf Norris, so if he was not busy we usually had to stay for a chat. The walk to my Aunt's must have been about three- quarters of a mile She lived in a tiny cottage at the end of a terrace in the old part of the town, bang next to the gasworks which had two gasometers and massive piles of coke with its distinctive smell. Despite this pong, there always seemed to be something happening in the works of interest to me. Another wonderful attraction was the small paddock at the back of the house, where the two youngest of my four male cousins would take me to play football. Fred was about twenty, Jack seventeen and they were kind to give time to a youngster like me. The cottage was really small and had only one room and a scullery downstairs. I recall that the open fire smoked badly and this, with the ever present smell of Uncle Albert's pipe, was a new experience. Romsey possessed no sewage system so the sanitation (!!!) was by means of a bucket in the privy at the top of a yard. Each night, so called "night soil carts" used to go around the town with men emptying these buckets from every house. Not an edifying job.

The Romsey Jam factory, run by Hattatt's who originally traded in Salisbury, was quite near my Aunt's house and she always seemed to have a large pile of discarded strawberry baskets of the woven wood type that had been discarded by the works, these were used to fuel the copper fire on wash days.

My Aunt excelled in cooking and I enjoyed her meals, so much so that on one occasion, I upset my mother when I asked why we couldn't have tea like the ones Aunt Rose produced. She explained that my aunt probably put on special shows for our visits. There was one frightening thing in the cottage, for over the fireplace was a framed, highly coloured print depicting Jacob's Ladder up to Heaven. At the top of the ladder were clouds and lots of angels; further down were people ascending, many falling off into a fiery pit which had horrible skeletons around it. Why anyone should want to give houseroom to such a monstrosity is beyond me. Between the fireplace and the window was a dresser with cupboards underneath and on this rested Uncle Albert's accordion. He fancied himself as an exponent of the instrument and we were never allowed to leave before enduring a rendering. He would sit in his armchair, wearing a soft smile with eyes almost closed, never seeming to bring forth a recognisable tune and it may seem unkind but I was always pleased when the rather embarrassing ordeal ended.

On one visit when I was about nine, I mentioned to Cousin Fred that my latest hobby was fretwork, and he said he thought that he still had a box of Hobbies Magazines and patterns. He went off to his bedroom and came back with a large cardboard box containing almost every issue from over an eighteen month period in 1915/16. That night, I struggled to the station, clutching my prize and spent a great deal of time in the next couple of years transforming those paper patterns into articles, using a simple hand saw. Relatives were showered with all sorts of gifts for Christmas and Birthdays, Letter Racks, Toast Racks, Pipe Racks, Jewel Boxes. I would save sixpence, then go to Hardy's, the Grocery Wholesalers in Brown Street, purchase a tea chest, carry it home (with many stops for rest), take it apart and I would have five good pieces of 3/16" three ply some two feet square all ready to commence operations. One sheet of the same size purchased at Pinders the Ironmongers cost ninepence at that time!

We had to allow plenty of time for the walk back to catch the train late in the evening. The station always seemed much more exciting when lit by the flickering gas lamps. The arrival of the train was heralded by Mr. Crabb shouting,

"Romsey — this is Romsey, change for the Andover line, change for the Andover line."

He never said where the train was going — I suppose the list of stations all the way to Cardiff was too much of an effort.

I was always pleased to get back to Salisbury even when I had enjoyed the day. The combined smells of the gasworks, the privy and smoky fire, together with Uncle Albert's pipe, were somewhat offputting.

20 "Biff" and "Bang"

After Easter, 1923, our whole class moved up a notch into Standard Two, the classroom on the other side of the dividing screen where we had Miss Judd as teacher. Now we really felt we counted for something, having left the bottom class, big enough even to be included in Mr. Russ's daily inspection each afternoon. This was somewhat of a mixed blessing as most of us fell foul of the Headmaster's constant campaign against dirty hands. Within a week or two, few of us had not suffered the indignity of "the biff" and his shouted instruction, "Go and wash." One event that took place during that first term is fixed firmly in my mind. During a Friday afternoon, it was a beautiful day in a hot summer, at about 2.45 pm the school was shaken by an explosion: we had heard nothing as loud before. Miss Judd said calmly,

"I wonder what that was?"

It seemed ages before four o'clock came round, as we were all anxious to get out from school to find what had happened. Alf Norris and I took our usual route, rather faster than most days, along Rampart Road, where we could see in the distance a large crowd gathered at the Milford Hill corner. We got there to learn that there had been a gas explosion at a house only twenty yards or so up the hill. We pushed our way through the crowd, the front of the house was a real shambles, the door had been blown off, all windows were gone and the ceilings were hanging in shreds. Then we realised that it was the Bean's house where Miss Judd lodged.

Apparently the Beans had reported the smell of gas, so two gas engineers arrived to find the leak. One of them struck a match and whomph, there was a terrific explosion. The only person injured was poor Mrs. Bean, who was ill for quite some time and when she died, only a few years later, it was said that her early death resulted from this occurrence. The aspidistra which she kept in the front window, was blown right across the street, a distance of perhaps forty feet and went through a large window in the house opposite. It was amazing that the two engineers escaped shaken but unhurt. Later that evening, poor Miss Judd had to climb a ladder to her bedroom, in full view of gaping crowds, to retrieve some of her clothes.

It was shortly after this that Dad came home to breakfast one morning to say that a man living in Dolphin Street and working as a porter at The Red Lion Hotel had attempted to cut his own throat. In the 'twenties, to try such a thing was a criminal act, so presumably the poor chap was dragged before magistrates. We used to pass along Dolphin Street on our way to and from school. Whenever we saw him we would slow up to stare and try to see if there was a scar on his throat.

In August of that year, Farrs had their one and only works outing. Dad took me with him and we went by Rowlands charabanc to Southampton, had dinner at Scotts Cafe down by the Pier, then by boat to Cowes. This was the first time that I had been on such a large ship, a paddle steamer called *The Lorna Doone* — a name to become famous only seventeen years later when she played a big part in the Dunkirk evacuation. I remember spending the whole time, both to and from the island, down in the engine room, watching the four huge pistons rising and falling, looking as though they would force their way through the piston blocks then quietly reach their peak and go in the opposite direction. The smell of hot oil fascinated me and whenever I have a whiff of it now am transported in my mind back to that first sea trip.

Just a week after my ninth birthday, I was awakened shortly after eight o'clock by my Aunt Gertrude, who told me to get up quickly, dress and go down to breakfast. As it was a Saturday, I wanted to know why she had not gone off to work as usual and got the reply "Mum's not very well." There seemed to be a great deal of activity, then a strange lady in nurse's uniform came and when she went upstairs, I began to worry that Mum must be very ill.

At nine o'clock, there was the cry of a baby and everyone started telling me that I had a baby sister, what did I think of that? The news stunned me, I already had two sisters, I often wished that I had a brother to play with, but another sister!! Then I was told to make myself scarce. I went off to see my friend, Alf Norris, and self- consciously told him the news at which he laughed. His mother went into raptures of delight whilst Alf spent the morning telling me that I would have to push the baby out in the pram and always look after her, making me somewhat down in the dumps.

When I got home, I was allowed to go and peep at my new sister laying in my old black cast-iron cot, which had been brought out to stand by Mum and Dad's bed. I had to admit that she looked quite nice, in fact very nice. So much so, that in my efforts to take a closer look I put my head through the bars at the end of the bed, then found that I was trapped. Dad had to be fetched and with the help of a length of wood, bent the bars sufficiently to release me. In one way, I did have cause to celebrate Margaret's arrival for no longer was I the baby of the family.

21 More About School

I remember two great disappointments experienced during the early part of 1924. The first when what should have been a great day instead turned out to be a very damp squibb. We were to hear wireless for the very first time. After all, the BBC had only made its first broadcast some eighteen months earlier and many of our elders still cast doubts as to whether the system could work.

Mr. Edwards and Mr. Shergold brought the receiver along to school where it was set up in the corner of Standard Six's classroom to be near the aerial. This was a massive affair of twin wires, held apart by battens about three feet in length and the whole concoction was stretched from the window to the top of the flagpole, halfway down the playground. The set itself seemed enormous, being about two feet six inches square with the works open for all to see. It contained numerous coils, made from cardboard tubes and had a dozen or so what looked like electric light bulbs but which we soon learned were radio valves. The name wireless was a misnomer for the table was covered in wires.

The set was switched on but not a sound came from the gramophone horn that turned out to be a loudspeaker. Mr. Edwards produced a box and then the two masters spent a considerable time removing valves, replacing with new ones, switching them around, making other adjustments, probably swearing under their breath, but still not a squeak. Never had the assembled school been so well behaved for the warnings of dire penalties if silence was broken had really worked.

Eventually they gave it up as a bad job and Mr. Russ said that it reminded him of Wolfe's poem, "The burial of Sir John Moore at Corunna": "Not a drum was heard not a bugle note". This remark brought loud laughter and eased the tension. The school then went to the playground for afternoon break and normal lessons followed.

The experience was not repeated, but later that year whilst on a half-day trip to London to see my uncle, I did hear radio for the first time. Uncle Arthur had bought a Brownie Crystal Set and, being only a few miles from Savoy Hill, the BBC Headquarters, got excellent reception. The set was encased in bakelite, an early plastic, measured some nine inches square and six inches high. The only outside wires were the aerial and earth connections, the cat's whisker and crystal being encased in a glass tube on top of the set. It really was a neat job and all you had to do was move the cat's whisker (a piece of very fine wire) around by means of a tiny handle at the left of the tube and find a sensitive spot on the crystal which was a type of quartz. You listened through headphones and immediately the sensitive spot was found, "Eureka!", you had a programme. Uncle had discovered that if he placed the headphones in a basin, then both he and my aunt could listen at the same time — was this the first amplifier?

The second disappointment was due to complete lack of care on the part of the organisers of a lecture for the city schoolchildren. The top four classes from our school marched to The Victoria Hall in Rollestone Street to hear a talk by no less a person than Sir Adrian Boult, the composer and conductor. The Victoria Hall, which held some four to five hundred people, belonged to The Salisbury Steam Laundry and, prior to the first World War, was used as a swimming bath in summer and a concert hall during the winter months.

Although music was not an interest of mine, I looked forward to this talk by such an eminent personality. A large slide screen had been erected on the stage and our school had excellent seats in the balcony. As soon as Sir Adrian started talking, I thought that we were in for a treat for within a few minutes he had shown how, with three simple notes, we could make a tune and had us all singing "Three Blind Mice". Then the great man tapped with his pointer for the first slide to be shown. The result was quite ludicrous for the organisers had forgotten that the hall had large roof lights and this was a bright afternoon. Against these the projector stood no chance, the screen was moved right to the rear of the stage but still no joy. The various headmasters went into conference with the speaker in full view of the audience. Things got rather heated and then he stumped off in a high dudgeon. A few minutes later we were given our marching orders and went home. It really was a shambles and a great pity for I recognised that Sir Adrian had a wonderful way of explaining the secret of music to children. It was small wonder that he was upset and did not come back on another occasion after this fiasco.

Looking back, I realise just how dedicated the teachers at Saint Martin's School were, even giving up a great deal of their own time in the evenings and holidays. One example of this dedication was the History Charts which they must have made during the Easter holidays, prior to the start of the new School Year. The charts measuring about fifteen feet in length, by two feet in height were fixed on the wall, behind and above the master's desk. They were divided into quarter centuries covering the period of history to be taught during the next three terms. We had the lesson and at the end the master had a previously prepared paper slip bearing the name of the event that we had been studying, together with the exact date all in block capitals about one inch high; these were beautifully produced by means of stencils. The school steps were fetched from the broom cupboard, the slip was pasted and the master mounted the steps and fixed the event and date in correct position. Thus, for the remainder of the year, the information so recorded was right in front of the class and so was easily assimilated. These days, the learning of historical dates is somewhat out of fashion but the use of these charts added interest to the subject and helped to drive the information home.

When we were in Standard Five, Mr. Ralph Shergold introduced the class to elementary electricity. He brought along a pair of shocking coils, a car battery and a rheostat, which controlled the amount of electricity passing through the coils. In the first experiment the whole class joined hands and the boy at either end of the chain held one of the coils. When Mr. Shergold switched on, at first with low power, only a tingling was felt in the hands. He then moved the rheostat gradually until we began to jump around and found that it was impossible to let go of our neighbour's hand. Then a bucket of water was obtained and old "Ralph" threw a load of pennies in and also one of the shocking coils. In turn, we braved the low charge of electricity, held the other coil in the left hand and retrieved a penny from the bottom of the bucket with the right.

We were allowed to keep the coins. Then he placed a silver half-a-crown in the bucket and called for volunteers to retrieve the valuable coin — equivalent in those days to a skilled man's wages for two hours.

One or two braver types stepped forward, pulled up their sleeves, clasped the coil in the left hand and made a quick grab, but old Ralph was too clever for them. As soon as their hands touched the water he put the rheostat handle over so that a full charge of electricity went through. Their hands got half way down the bucket and they then found an invisible vice was holding them. It was all good fun and most instructive — it was an off the curriculum lesson which Mr. Shergold must have paid for. Apart from the 35-40 pennies which we kept, he had hired the equipment. He had a strict side but only caned on few occasions.

I well remember the Thursday afternoon when he gave me four of the best but it was well deserved. We were going through a craze of flicking ink-soaked pellets of blotting paper at the boys in the front rows. It was my misfortune to flick and flick hard, just as Ralph stopped walking up the gangway towards his desk and turned. To my horror, the pellet rose to a fair height and hit him on the right cheek producing a real splotch. Of course loud laughter from the rest of the class.

"Who did that?"

I put up my hand, knowing that I was for the high jump,

"Right, go into Standard Four and fetch my cane that Mr. Simmonds borrowed this morning."

Off I went, made the request to "Simmy", to be questioned in stage whispers by those in the front row,

"Who's it for — you?"

I just nodded, went back into Standard Five and Ralph caned me on the right hand, then the left, right again completing the quartet on the left. It hurt because he stood six feet three inches and as I was only about four feet ten — the cane came down a long way. It made no difference to the high regard that I always had for him because I knew it was my fault and could expect punishment.

The one and only time I thought Mr. Shergold was being unfair occurred during a Geometry lesson. The previous day we had Geography and he had impressed into our fat heads that one degree of longitude was about 69 miles. The Geometry lesson was about circles and he said that a circle contained 360 degrees, then asked what was one degree? With others, I put up my hand but was not asked to give the answer, one after another my colleagues told Ralph that one degree was 69½miles. I kept on sticking up my hand, saying "Sir, Sir" but was still ignored. Eventually the noise that I was making brought on my head, the frustration that he was experiencing,

"Maidment, if you don't stay quiet, I shall cane you."

Whilst I went quiet and felt so hard done by, once more he explained to the class that there were 360 degrees in a circle, so what was one degree? He asked round the class, still getting the answer of 69 miles. Eventually he said,

"Maidment, will you tell them."

"One degree is a three hundred and sixtieth part of a circle, Sir."

My friends around me realised what clots they'd been and I was not too popular, with the result that after that episode, sometimes when I did know the answer, I stayed quiet rather than show my colleagues up. Sometimes it is better to hide your light under a bushel!

On the opposite side of St. Martin's Church Street, some fifty to sixty yards from the school was Mrs. Burden's shop. This was run in the front room of what was a small cottage, the shop no more than eight feet square. Although the front door was always open, the shop door to the right of the passage was locked. Mrs. Burden's was well patronised by the children from both the Infants' and Boys' Schools. If you wanted to buy something, you just stood in the passage by the shop door and pulled a string which rang an old-fashioned bell in the nether regions of the house. After an interval, Mrs. Burden would appear and, being almost as big round as she was tall, seemed to completely fill the passage from wall-to-wall. She shuffled along toward you, in her carpet slippers, fumbling for her keys beneath her massive skirt.

In later years, I often wondered whether her efforts could have been worthwhile, for often we only went in to spend a ha'penny. Walter, her husband, was a bit of a rough diamond, who scratched a living by touring the City streets and surrounding villages with a small flat cart drawn by a donkey. His raucous shout of "Rag-a-bone" was a familiar sound, as was his shouting at Saint Martin's Football Team's home matches where he was looked upon as something of a cheer-leader. I can recall his stentorian voice, no doubt kept in training by his job, shouting "Up the Saints!" or "Keep it on the Island!", if the ball was booted into touch.

My friend Alf Norris and I used to go home together and passed, on the corner of Rampart Road with Southampton Road, Armitage's Iron

Works, called "The Saint Ann's Foundry". It had closed down late in 1922 and remained so for some ten or twelve years. In its heyday the works had been well known, and examples of the castings produced can still be seen in the City. We used to look through windows which year by year became more and more grimy and cobweb-encrusted. Everything had been left as though the workers had just gone home for the night, tools and materials on the benches getting increasingly rusty as the rain dripped onto them through a leaking roof. It was quite a creepy looking place and not the only one in Rampart Road for, some sixty yards from Armitage's, was what we called "The Haunted House". It had been empty for several years and although here again windows were covered with cobwebs and dust, it still looked in good condition for it was never vandalised. Rumours abounded — it was haunted — we were told stories of ghosts, so that we always crossed to the other side of the road and ran past.

The truth, so I was told many years later, was that the owner who lived alone, had been killed in action during the First World War, leaving no apparent heirs and so the house remained empty for about fifteen years. During the whole of that time it attracted no squatters, nor was it vandalised. How different today!

Towards the end of that section of Rampart Road was Percy's Dairy, owned by Mr. John Percy — a large red-faced man with ginger hair and moustache. He was always to be seen, nonchalantly driving his horse-drawn milk float. Unfortunately, one day in 1922 the animal bolted, the float overturned and Mr. Percy was killed. I remember wondering how such a big man could possibly die in this way. My mother thought highly of him, for when churchwarden of St. Martin's, he went house to house around the parish collecting for the poor victims of a fire in Dolphin Street who had no insurance.

22 *Soccer Mad*

I've had a passion for football since I was about six. My early games in the Infants' School playground were played with a tennis ball in deadly serious fashion, but after going into the Boys' School in 1922, every Saturday from September until April, weather permitting, was spent at Shady Bower or occasionally, the Green Croft. Usually there was someone who was the proud owner of a football. We played with a variety of sizes, sometimes even with a full-size ball, which was a bit too much for seven-year-olds.

Footballs had to be frequently inflated or, as we said, "blown-up". This meant a visit to Mr. Eminton in Winchester Street. He was a bootmaker, living just below the Guilder Lane corner and had all the equipment we needed for the job: a pump with special adaptor, the string to tie the bladder and a large packing needle with wooden handle for lacing the case. We trooped, not more than three at the time, into the front room used as his workshop, paid the old gentleman one penny and this allowed us use of the tools kept in a box in the far corner. Although we did our best to blow up the ball it was invariably without much success, whereupon Mr. Eminton would offer to help, which meant he did the job. However he always kept an ear open for his wife, a large lady whereas he was quite short. Should he hear her footsteps coming down the passage, the ball would be quickly passed to us and he continued with his bootmaking. He was kind and I expect our visits enlivened his day.

Sometimes we were reduced to a football case, minus a bladder. Our remedy was to stuff it with newspaper. If you've never kicked such a ball, my advice is don't, it's heavy as lead and you feel as if you've broken your leg.

Most of us were football mad and though denied the modern child's benefit of televised matches, we would watch the Saint Martin's side every other Saturday. We did our best to mimic our heroes and I remember how John Tiller, my friend, would say, "I'm Aubrey Searle." He was the Saints captain and centre-half, had been born with a deformed foot which gave him a slight limp, so John also played with a limp. There was the time that George Searle, Aubrey's brother, played wearing a black knee bandage. We were convinced that this must make you able to play better, so we had to have some, which meant that a pair of my sister's old black school stockings were chopped up and several of us followed George's example. Unfortunately, the stockings were sizes too large so the surplus was taken up by using safety pins.

Our games always brought arguments about the interpretation of the rules and there were those who became self-proclaimed experts. Invariably the opinions offered favoured their own side and usually these legal experts got it all wrong. One of these was Arthur Cook, who never expected to be contradicted for was not his Uncle Fred the well known St. Martin's outside-right? One week we were really foxed to read in *The Salisbury Times* that Charlie Wigley, the Saints inside-forward, had scored a hat trick. A wiseacre in our group said that it only meant he was wearing a cap whilst scoring a goal. We thought this must be true for what else could it mean?

Should St. Martin's have a match in the afternoon, we were warned off the pitch and could only use the remaining space on the two sides bordering the railway. Unfortunately the ball was sometimes kicked over or through the wire-stranded fence and would then roll down to the railway lines. It was an unwritten law that the last kicker was first fetcher, but woe betide him if caught by one of the many railwaymen working there. Then the air would become blue with alternative language — wonderful training for small boys, but these tellings-off were well deserved as a great deal of shunting was always in progress at the Goods Station, whilst around the corner was the main Salisbury-Southampton line. Fortunately, no tragedies occurred, whether by good fortune or because we became extremely wary as a result of the constant remonstrations is anyone's guess.

Shady Bower's other snag was the steel-spiked railings bordering the remaining two sides of the field. It was amazing the number of times that footballs would fall vertically on the top of these — loud hisses would follow and the balls sat deflated on the spikes. I could never understand why it did not occur to anyone to either cut the points off or bend them over, as they were no longer a deterrent to trespassers, for rails had been bent in several places to allow all but the most corpulent to squeeze through.

The Saint Martin's team of the 'twenties was the premier local junior side, winning everything in sight, including The Wiltshire Junior Cup three times. The bringing home of a trophy to the Clubrooms in Milford Hill was always a tremendous occasion with supporters in high spirits filling the street. In the 'twenties television was unknown and, as few people possessed a radio before the end of the decade, there was little alternative entertainment, and it was amazing how many people followed the Saints. A crowd of two to three hundred was quite normal and an admission charge of fourpence was made. It was a bone of contention that far too many watched from outside the fence in Shady Bower Road, so a bright individual had a flash of genius. Posts some seven feet in height were erected just inside the railings and a hessian screen was strung between them on match days. Whether the effort involved was too much or because match receipts remained the same, for some reason the scheme was quickly abandoned.

In 1923, spectators became so numerous and were standing so close to the touchlines that the Wiltshire Football Association ordered that the pitch should be roped off. A deadline was given for the work to be completed and I remember that team members were still driving in posts on the morning of a match and were still attaching ropes to these just prior to kick-off. I wonder why they left the job to the last moment.

The Shady Bower pitch was far from being a smooth piece of turf for nothing in the way of improvement had been done from the time that a former Rector had purchased the field in the early years of the century. The two goal areas and the centre circle were totally devoid of grass even at the start of the season. After a few wet days these became mud patches, which meant the leather-cased balls became heavier and heavier as the game progressed. How different to the present when plastic cases mean the ball is the same weight both at the beginning and end of a match.

From the playing point of view the Bower had a real drawback, which opponents reckoned was worth a goal start to the home side. The corner surrounded by the Railway was some two to three feet lower than the goal area which meant that wingers would find the ball running away from them and the goal area appeared to them to be at waist level. Most local pitches did however have similar faults to rather even things up.

When St. Martin's played Fussells the games were real local derbies, not the place for faint-hearted players as they were quite physical encounters but never dirty. I do not recall anyone being cautioned, let alone sent off.

It was a man's game, fair shoulder charges with hard tackling. Passing back to the goalkeeper was almost unknown; in the mud of the Bower, this modern timewaster could have proved dangerous for the defending team as most likely the ball would have stuck in the mire. The two teams always looked resplendent — the Saints in their unusual black shirts and white shorts while Fussells had red shirts, again with white shorts.

Gates for these games would be anything up to five hundred and spectators had talking points for weeks to come.

Four or five of the Saints players had spent the entire war in India as members of The 4th Battalion, Wiltshire Regiment and had thus played together for some time. This nucleus formed the basis of what became an excellent team which later provided the Wiltshire County Senior side with four players: Len Brown — a goalkeeper who despite massive build was most agile; Jack Edgington — a classic full back; Charlie or "Cheddar" Rattue — a terrier of a half-back; and Johnny Hill — a stalwart centre-half. Added to these were Aubrey and George Searle, the latter went on to high honours as a Football League referee and was a linesman at the 1947 Cup Final at Wembley. Amongst other players of the era were Charlie Read, Fred Cook, Ernie Walliker, Charlie Wigley and Reverend Ernest Cross. This last gentleman, a tutor at Salisbury Theological College, was almost a giant, well-built and about six foot three inches tall. However, he had a weakness, often displayed in the mud of Shady Bower, for he used to go up to a great height, head the heavy ball, then collapse like a log. I do hope his efforts did not have a lasting effect in later life.

On one occasion when the reverend gentleman was playing for the Saints at Royal Air Force Station, Old Sarum, he objected to the foul language being used by spectators supporting the home side, complained first to the referee, then made an official complaint to the County Association. I sympathise with him for I well remember in my

The Saint Martin's side of 1923/24, almost their last season of success. Several players were now well into their thirties but they had enjoyed five wonderful years:
Back Row: Farmer (trainer), Mortimer, Scott, Read, G.Searle, Adams, House, Fulford, Shipsey and Marks;
Front Row: Moore, Crutcher, Wigley, A.Searle (Captain), Walliker, Williamson, Cook and Lapham;
The diminutive Mr Lapham at the right of the front row was scorer during the cricket season (see page 147).

own playing days when opposing The Royal Artillery, Porton team, their linesman, a staff sergeant, was urging his players to "kill the bastards". This was heard by the referee who relieved him of his flag and reported the matter to the Wiltshire Association.

Returning to Shady Bower, the pavilion although brick built with corrugated iron roof was, to say the least, primitive. It had no water supply and the privy at the rear was furnished with a bucket that was seldom emptied. Even so it compared well with the facilities at other grounds with the exception of the playing fields enjoyed by Service teams which included Royal Air Force Stations at Old Sarum, Netheravon and Upavon, The Balloon School at Rollestone, The Royal Artillery and Royal Engineers at Porton and Royal Artillery, Larkhill.

I must admit to envy when I see the difference that sixty years has brought for junior football — mown pitches with showers available after the match. It's a different world, but I'm sure the standard of play has not gone up as a result. We were fitter, practiced harder and beer and cigarettes were not on the menu. I have seen in recent years, players going into the local, just prior to a match — how they expect to last ninety minutes after a pint or two is beyond my comprehension.

Occasionally I used to go with Dad to watch the two senior teams — Salisbury City and Salisbury Corinthians — at Victoria Park. Until 1924, City were in The Hampshire League, Corinthians in The Wiltshire League, but then the latter also went over to Hampshire, a move which prompted exciting local derbies, twice a year. However, in 1928, City joined the expanding Western League, bringing clubs with quite unknown names to the Park — Welton Rovers, Paulton Rovers and many others. The standard in this league was generally of a higher grade than either Hampshire or Wiltshire. The Corinthian sides usually contained several Old Wordsworthians including "Gip" Hinxman, who captained the Wiltshire County side at left back, Freddy Batt, a speedy winger who later became Salisbury's Mayor and Bob Inglefield, whose playing career as a wing half was cruelly cut short when he sustained a broken leg in one of the local derbies against "The City" on Easter Monday, 1927. He walked with quite a limp for the rest of his life! Two other stalwarts from B.W.S. were Sid and Teddy Larcombe. I remember my horror on hearing the news on a Sunday morning in the Spring of 1923 that Teddy, Corinthians goalkeeper, had the previous afternoon dived at the feet of an onrushing Portland United forward, sustained a fractured skull and died before reaching hospital at Weymouth. Soccer does not have many fatal accidents to players and this occurrence shocked the community for Teddy was a popular team member.

For normal games, admission to the Park was free to boys under fourteen, but the rule was changed without notice on an occasion when Wiltshire played Sussex in The Southern Counties Amateur League in 1924. My two friends and I were most keen to see the game, as

Wiltshire had included F.N.S.Creek, a schoolmaster at Dauntsey College and an England Amateur International who had recently received a full International Cap when he played against France. This was the very first time that such a celebrity had played in Salisbury so we set off very early to see the game.

During the long walk, our pocket money was spent on sweets to sustain us during the match, so we were shocked to see a sign stating "Boys 3d" hung on the one paybox. We tried to sidle past, but were stopped by the shout of,

"Can't you boys read?"

We then conferred and my two friends said,

"Let's go round to Park Lane and take a hedge ticket."

Park Lane was at the far end of the ground and for the uninitiated a "hedge ticket" meant squeezing through the hedge without payment. My own nerve failed me, so off I went to scrounge the admission price from Mum, then run back again (it was a two mile round trip) before the kick-off. When I returned to the Park, there was no sign of my friends and I learned later they had been spotted as they went through the hedge and threatened with Police action. I recollect that when Wiltshire came on to the pitch, Creek was walking nonchalantly with both hands in pockets at the sides of his shorts. This was the first time I had seen anyone wearing shorts having side pockets and in my mind placed him in a high category of his own. Unfortunately, Wiltshire were up the creek, losing by five goals to two.

As far as my own playing career was concerned, this started at the age of nine, when only two weeks after being enrolled as a Wolf Cub, I had my first competitive match in the Wolf Cub League for 15th Salisbury St. Martin's Pack. This match against St. Thomas' was played on The Fairfield beyond Victoria Park. The field now houses Waters and Fairfield Roads. We lost more games than we won until the 1925/26 season when were were undefeated. During that year, in the match against 5th Salisbury (United Methodist) I had the good fortune to score all four goals in our 4-2 win and spent the rest of that week-end in the seventh heaven of delight because a classmate, Tubby Mortimer, already a member of the school team at the age of eleven, was one of the 5ths stalwarts. Arriving at school on the Monday morning, my friends enquired how we got on:

"Won 4-2".

"Did you score any?", came the reply.

"Yes, all four."

Whereupon Tubby who was nearby and still smarting after the defeat said,

"All he does is wait near the goal and soon as he gets the ball he puts it in."

I've thought of that remark many times and surely scoring goals is the prime reason for the game. Those cub matches were as keenly fought as any senior game and it was ideal preparation for the years ahead.

At school, we had the House system, the houses being Saxons, Normans, Britons, Celts and Angles. I was in the latter team and got my first game when I was ten. Fortune smiled on me that afternoon for the opposing goalkeeper came out of goal, fielded the ball and, instead of kicking cleanly up the field, sliced it sideways and it came in a lovely arc towards me, playing on the left-wing. As it dropped, I gave the ball an almighty wallop and it fell gently behind the keeper into goal before he had a chance to get back. This fluke turned out to be the only goal of the game and though I became the hero of the hour, never let on that I had not intended it to be a shot.

Competition in the Inter-schools League was very keen, the matches always being played on Thursday afternoons at Victoria Park. In my first year at The Boys' School we had an excellent team, won the league and supplied two players for the Salisbury Boys' Team — Doug Stanley at centre forward and Arthur Bligh at right-half. Unfortunately, after a creditable 2-2 draw at Victoria Park against Oxford Boys they lost the replay by 6-2.

After that year the school team was no great shakes and I remember that in 1925, following a seven nil defeat by St. Edmund's there was quite a furore and Sammy Edwards, the master in charge of football, threatened to cane the entire team if there was a repeat of such a disgraceful performance. In the event he never did but he was quite capable of doing it.

Despite this it was every boy's dream to play for the school wearing our red and white striped jerseys. Unfortunately I never made it, for at the age of eleven I left to go to Bishop Wordsworth's School. In later years, I captained a Saints' side in The Salisbury and District League but that's another story.

23 *I Join the Cubs*

For quite a long time I had wanted to join The Wolf Cubs, but rather stupidly listened to the scorn poured on the idea by my school friend, Alf Norris.

However, on a Saturday morning in the Spring of 1923, my mother saw Miss Joyce Brown, the Saint Martin's Cub Mistress walking along the street, had a word with her, then called me. Miss Brown was massively built, nearly six feet tall and most unusually for those days had her hair cut short in a rather mannish style. She lived with her father, the Rev. Claude Brown, a frail old gentleman in his eighties and a retired clergyman who had been Vicar of Verwood in Dorset. Their home, Milford Hill House, had earlier belonged to a banking family and possessed extensive grounds. Miss Brown fed me with the correct bait to gain my interest,

"Did I play football?"

When I said, "Yes", she replied,

"Would you like to play in a practice match this afternoon?"

How could I refuse? I went along and played in the match held in Mr. & Mrs. Sargeant's field in Shady Bower Road. They put me in goal and although we lost, made several saves which seemed to please the rest of the team. After the match we paddled in a small stream at the edge of the field and I found that I was on the way to becoming a Wolf Cub.

On the following Friday, I attended the Pack Meeting at the Gigant Street Room and was told to meet Hughie Easen, the other new recruit the next morning so that we could go to the Scout Shop over the Midland Bank in the Cheese Market to collect our uniforms. The shop, only open on Saturday mornings, was manned by Miss Queenie Jones, the Cub Mistress of the 6th Salisbury, St. Paul's Pack. We were quickly fitted with blue jerseys and shorts, green caps with yellow piping and given our 15th Salisbury scarves of green and brown. I remember as soon as we reached the street we put on the caps, feeling very self-conscious about it, but I don't suppose anyone noticed. The following Friday, Hugh and I were duly sworn-in as Wolf Cubs at a special service held at St. Mary Magdalene's Church in Gigant Street. We made our Cub Promises, then Miss Brown pinned the various badges and shoulder flashes to our uniforms, to be sewn on later. We then joined the sixes to which we had been designated, I went in the Red Six and had as Sixer, Les Ranger. I stayed in the Cubs until nearly twelve when I became a Scout for five years, leaving at seventeen with the rank of Troop Leader. That was not however the end, as for the next eighteen months I helped the Troop as unofficial Assistant Scout Master.

On Easter Sunday, ten days after my enrollment, we had Church Parade, my first public appearance in uniform. Our Pack Flag, with the Union Jack, was carried by a colour party and placed by the altar. After the service we paraded on the church forecourt for inspection by The Rector and Churchwardens. Each sixer called his six to alert — we came to attention, endeavouring to stand rigidly, not an easy matter for small boys. I expect it looked a pantomime but it was a milestone in my life, the church parades of later years were never so frightening as that one.

During that summer we paid two visits to Wilton Park, the first to play The 1st Wilton Pack at cricket. We met at The Gigant Street Room, then marched to The Great Western Railway Station where we entrained for Wilton. Arriving there, we had to march to Wilton House,

The Great Western Railway Station (opposite the Postal Sorting Office) where we "entrained for Wilton". It was closed for Passenger Traffic in 1925.

so that before the match started we had already walked two and a half miles. Needless to say we lost, but had a jolly good time with tea on the lawn. The Wilton cubmistress was the Earl of Pembroke's daughter and let us paddle in the river by the famous Palladian Bridge. The water, even on that lovely summer day was quite cold and Lady Patricia Herbert said that it was due to the very fast flow of the River Nadder.

In August we had a Salisbury and District Wolf Cubs' Cricket Tournament at the same venue. Each pack entered three players and all those not batting, fielded. A most peculiar method of scoring was used — the runs scored counted for your pack; if you bowled someone out you scored two; if a batsman was caught, both bowler and fielder got one point. I managed to bowl two and one was caught from my bowling and, though I was run out without receiving a ball, I returned home feeling that I had done my bit for 15th Salisbury.

The first hurdle a tenderfoot had to tackle were the tests for "first-star", ten in number. I quickly passed nine but then came a mighty stumbling block — skip thirty backwards. My co-ordination at skipping was woeful to say the least and I suffered the indignity of younger and newer recruits passing me in the race for that first star. I had already passed most of the second-star tests before something clicked — it was almost Easter a year later when suddenly I discovered that I could skip. Within a week thirty was a doddle, I could do a hundred. Shortly after I was wearing both first and second stars in my cap and promotion to second in the six meant that I also now had a yellow stripe on my right arm to indicate rank.

We spent many afternoons on Laverstock Down, the sun always seemed to be shining, tracking was one of the main pastimes and competition between the four sixes was intense. We lit fires on the lee side of the clump of trees at the top of the down and the food we cooked always seemed better than that eaten at home. Those same trees provided hours of pleasure, climbing until really tired, then suddenly realising that we had a two and a half mile trek home.

After obtaining the second star you became eligible to work for proficiency badges, these numbered twelve and every one obtained meant a ribbon carrying your name was attached to the totem pole below that particular badge. The badges were always presented at either the Easter or Christmas Church Parades which became quite big occasions for us. In 1925 I really worked hard to pass the badge tests and at Christmas was presented with seven at the same time. Walking home from church after The Rector had pinned them to my jersey, my right arm seemed to weigh a ton. I remember them now — Athlete, Footballer, Carpenter, Artist, Guide, House Orderly and First Aid.

Miss Brown was helped by Miss Christine Gordon, who was an unofficial Assistant Cub Mistress, she never wore uniform. A very gentle lady, she had served in The Red Cross in France during the war and was an excellent teacher of First Aid, the bandaging she taught me has proved of use time and time again during the sixty five years that have passed since that time.

A Cubs' Athletic Meeting was held during the School Holidays of 1924. It was a boiling hot day and all the local packs marched to a field just below Bouverie Avenue on the Coombe Road. Miss Ellis, the District Commissioner (known as "Pecker" because of her large nose) was in charge and made all the arrangements. She too was a well built lady, had a perpetual smile and was really kind. She obtained permission to use the field but could not have made a visit of inspection, for when we all arrived we found the grass was about two feet high. Athletics were out, there was lots of moaning but in any case it was a hot day and most of us were already tired after the long tramp.

24 Out in the Sticks

One of my father's best friends was Mr. Tom Bussell, who had worked with him as a coachbuilder at Farr's before the war. He joined The Royal Engineers in 1915 and after demobilisation in 1919, went back to his old job, staying with my family until he was able to find accommodation. That enabled his wife and four year old son, Bill, to join him. Housing just after the First World War being extremely difficult, he was forced to make do with two furnished rooms at a house in York Road.

It was over a year later that eventually the Bussells were able to find a house and had to move two miles from the City Centre to Church Road, Laverstock, only about 150 yards from St. Thomas' Bridge. There was no regular bus service so Mr. Bussell did as so many of his contemporaries were forced to do — cycled to and from work. This was not a problem during daylight hours, but at that time cycle lighting was still somewhat primitive as either oil or acetylene gas lamps were the only ones available. Electric battery or dynamo types were several years in the future. Few people had rear lamps and reflectors were unknown so that a ride at night through country roads in foul weather was really hazardous. The only blessing was that motor traffic was light.

A daughter was born to the Bussells in 1921 and I spent many happy days with the family. The Silver Star Bus Company began a morning and evening service for workers at The Porton Experimental Station, which in those early days was mainly a collection of corrugated iron huts. The bus, which really looked a Silver Star with its coachwork of polished aluminium, left The Blue Boar Row in Salisbury at about 8.30 am and I returned with the workers at 5.30 pm for a fare of tuppence each way.

Laverstock really was in the country. There were few houses beyond The London Road Cemetery and, apart from their immediate neighbours, the Bussells were quite isolated though this had its compensations for two small boys. The River Bourne ran alongside the garden and immediately adjoining St. Thomas' Bridge, the wide ford made an excellent paddling pool. Opposite this was a chalk pit so useful for climbing and at the corner with the main London Road a tiny cottage, at one time probably a toll house, was seldom inhabited, giving it an air of mystery. Along the road was a very friendly farmer, who allowed us to take short cuts through his yard, leading to a steep climb up to the clump of trees at the top of Laverstock or as it was known locally, Cocky Down. Some two hundred yards from the clump was Pug's Hole which I would think was some thirty feet across and of about the same depth. The trees growing in this did not poke their heads much above the surrounding land and we used to speculate as to how and why the hole was there at all.

In the 1920's, St. Thomas' Bridge was the scene of innumerable fatal accidents. Traffic would gather speed coming down the long uninterrupted Three Mile Hill and the drivers would be suddenly faced with having to negotiate the humpbacked stone bridge, built at an angle of 45 degrees to the approach road. Brakes in those days were not too efficient, so that invariably they would not be able to take the bend and so careered through the parapet to The River Bourne below.

St Thomas' Bridge at Laverstock in 1920. It remained a death-trap for unwary motorists until rebuilding in 1935. Note the "Toll-House" in the background.

The bridge became so notorious that The Royal Automobile Club set up a manned box on the corner of Church Lane. Bill and I became very friendly with the patrolman, Mr. Crouch, a retired Sergeant of The Wiltshire Constabulary, who would arrive each morning in stately fashion on his motor-bike with the attached box-like sidecar which carried all his tools. He would spend the rest of the daylight hours on point duty, the traffic density bore no resemblance to the present day for he always seemed to have time to pop back to his box between the signalling of vehicles. He was a cheerful type — big and beefy with the typical heavy moustache of the period. We would sit in the box with him, he was always ready with a story that he told with one ear cocked. At the sound of a car coming down the hill, he slowly wandered out, stood a yard or two into the road to signal the driver to slow and would then wave him on. The very sight of this large ex-policeman probably saved a number of lives.

On a couple of occasions, The Courtenay Tracey Otterhounds hunted The Bourne and Bill and I followed on foot, getting pretty wet and dirty. I remember the huntsmen, in their dark green coats with white breeches and quite peculiar hats, carrying a strange sort of crook. Even as a small boy, I thought that it was a strange overrated pastime and never saw them catch an otter.

In 1923, Flying Officer and Mrs. Parker took rooms in the Bussell's house. He was, at that time, the Radio Officer at Royal Air Force, Old Sarum and went to and from the station on a 250 cc motorbike. He built and installed a radio receiver at home and the first broadcast that I ever heard through a loudspeaker came from this set late in 1924. It seemed like magic to hear the service direct from St. Martin's-in-the-Fields in London and I well remember the hymn that was sung, "Praise my soul, the King of Heaven".

Mr. Parker left the Air Force in 1925, was a very keen and successful fisherman and would pay Bill and I to collect tins of worms for him. Later they took The Bull public house at Downton and turned it into a fishing hotel that became famous nationwide.

There was one big snag about the Bussell's house, the lavatory was in a small detached stable at the rear and invariably there were rats around — the river was only a few yards away. After dark, the only illumination available was a candle lamp and it was a bit scary to hear the creatures scuttle away. I am still not very fond of them.

25 *The End of an Era*

Easter, 1926 was quite a significant time for me. Firstly, I was due to go up into Standard Six to be taught by the rather frightening Sammy Edwards. During the previous two years, I had been in Mr. Ralph Shergold's class. To be taught by the same teacher for two successive years was a unique occurrence and only came about because the previous Easter, Mr. Windust had taken up the Headship of a Boys' School at Weymouth, Sammy Edwards moved up to take Windy's classes and Ralph Shergold moved up from Standard Four to Five. A new master, Mr. Simmonds, a fine athlete, came to take over Standard Four. Those two years spent under Ralph had been extremely happy so I was saddened to leave him.

Secondly, in March I had taken the first two parts of the Grammar School Entrance Examinations (later to become the eleven plus). They were held at our School over two successive days, on the first morning we had Mathematics, Part I and the afternoon was taken up with English Part I. On the next day we had the second part of both subjects. The examination was compulsory for all reaching the age of eleven between September 1925 and August 1926. When the results came through, whilst I was pleased to head the list with an overall 90%, 216 marks from 240, my reaction was somewhat muted for I was not sure that I wished to go on to The Bishop Wordsworth's School. Dad and Mum wanted me to take the Scholarship Exams, to be held at the end of May as both my elder sisters had won places in their turn and though neither parent put pressure on me, I was well aware of what was expected.

When we started the new term, I soon discovered that Sammy Edwards was exactly as everyone had warned — a good teacher but given to bursts of violent temper. Only some five feet seven inches tall he was a real Jekyll and Hyde character, going from charm one moment to raging outburst the next. When I arrived in Standard Six, I was only 11½years of age and, as he took both Six and Seven, so I had, if I stayed at St. Martins until school leaving age, to look forward to almost three years under his tutelage.

It was precisely this thought that made up my mind about The Bishop's School. One Thursday morning, toward the end of April, the final lesson was taken up making pencil drawings of a wooden box which had the lid raised to reveal three compartments inside. It was a good exercise in perspective, I was quite pleased with my outline drawing and had just started shading when suddenly I received a terrific blow to my right ear. Sammy had come up behind from the back of the class and had given me a clout that left my head ringing for the rest of the lesson. He shouted. "That's not shading, that's just scribbling."

At the end of the morning, my mind was made up, I just could not countenance Sammy for three more years, so ran home, blurted out to Mum that Yes, I did want to take the Scholarship exam. Neither parent asked what had brought about this sudden change of heart. I told no-one and was quite proud that Sammy had not brought one tear.

The exams at Bishop Wordsworth's School were held on two successive Saturday mornings. The first was taken up with written work — Maths and English, the latter including a long piece of dictation. This, taken from Robert Louis Stevenson's *Treasure Island* was made difficult, for it was read by Mr. MacFarlane, the senior English master who spoke with a pronounced Scots burr. The following Saturday was mostly written work followed by individual oral examination by Mr. Reuben Bracher, the Headmaster.

One evening in early July, I was playing in a House Cricket Match at Shady Bower, when my eldest sister, Gertrude, who had just completed her second year at Bristol University, came cycling through the gates in great excitement. A letter had just arrived to say that I had been awarded a scholarship. Everyone made a great fuss of me, whilst I wondered what might have happened if Sammy Edwards had not tried to knock my head off.

During that May, the country was almost brought to a standstill by the General Strike which started on Tuesday May 4th and was called off on the 12th. It did not affect Salisbury as much as the larger towns and cities — there were few local trade unionists, with the exception of railwaymen. Whilst most of these went on strike, some continued to work and, though there was no violence, had to pass through picket lines to the shouts of 'scab'. The strike started in the mining industry and Dad sympathised with them, but could not understand why the comparatively well-paid railwaymen tried to hold the country to ransom.

The miners really did have a case - for several years we had seen almost daily, the plight of men as they passed through Salisbury, making their way on foot from South Wales to Southampton in the vain hope of finding work. They would go slowly along the streets singing away, (many of them had excellent voices), cap in hand hoping for a copper or two with which to buy a meal. The singing was essential if they were not to be charged with begging and though no-one had much spare cash, generally their efforts did not go unrewarded. Those who could not afford to give pennies, gave in kind, either food or a can of tea. It was a tragic sight, for some of those men driven to despair by years of unemployment, were forced to seek work in far away places and make the journey without money for fares or sustenance.

The summer term carried on much as usual and I was sorry as time elapsed to be leaving St. Martin's and my friends, most of whom I had known for almost nine years. I knew that from the next term, I would become in their eyes a "Bishop bulldog", and that relationships would be different.

The last afternoon arrived all too quickly and, at the end of term assembly, those boys who were leaving had to line up in front of the Headmaster's dais. Four of us were to go on to Bishop Wordsworth's — George Fulford and I won scholarships, Phil Mealing and Ted Haskell were to enter as fee paying pupils — two guineas, or two pounds, two shillings, a term. Mr. Russ went along the line, shook hands with each of us, wishing us well, then called on the school for a cheer. So my time, a happy time, at the school came to an end. Alf Norris and I took our well-worn path along St. Martin's Church Street across St. Ann's Street into Rampart Road. I remember we were both quiet and as we reached the Milford Hill corner, stopped and stood, hardly knowing what to say. Then Alf broke the ice with,

"Well, we shan't be doing this walk any more."

We wished one another "all the best" then in manly fashion made our way, Alf to his Greencroft Street home, whilst I slowly made my way down the hill to turn into Culver Street as I had done for the past eight years. It was the end of an era and brings me to the end of my book.